Choice, Chance & Organizational Change

Choice, Chance & Organizational Change

Practical Insights From Evolution for Business Leaders & Thinkers

Clay Carr

amacom
American Management Association

New York • Atlanta • Boston • Chicago • Kansas City • San Francisco • Washington, D.C.
Brussels • Mexico City • Tokyo • Toronto

Library of Congress Cataloging-in-Publication Data

Carr, Clay, 1934–
     Choice, chance & organizational change : practical insights from
evolution for business leaders & thinkers / Clay Carr.
        p.   cm.
     Includes bibliographical references and index.
     ISBN 0-8144-0279-8
     1. Organizational change.   2. Management.   3. Chief executive
officers.   4. Evolution (Biology)   5. Social Darwinism.
I. American Management Association.   II. Title.
HD58.8.C36317   1996
658.4'06—dc20   95-50416
                                                                      CIP

Printing number

10   9   8   7   6   5   4   3   2   1

Contents

Choice, Chance & Organizational Change

Introduction: Of Biology and Business

A revolution occurred in Western civilization in 1859. In that year, Charles Darwin published his *Origin of Species.* The book presented the idea of evolution—but that was hardly new. Philosophers all over the world had advanced this idea in one form or another for at least 2,400 years before Darwin. What made Darwin's view of evolution different was the process he described—evolution by means of natural selection from random mutations. And therein lies a relevant message for business in our own time.

For centuries before Darwin, virtually everyone thought that the world was a well-ordered place. If humans couldn't know the future, it was only because God had not revealed it. Because the universe was orderly, human kingdoms should be orderly—and they could be. This order was embodied in the wise emperor, king, or prince, who organized and led his kingdom so as to reflect the essential order of the universe.

Does that perhaps sound like our traditional view of corporate organization? It should, because our ideas are descended from these. Organizations today are minor variations on this theme: The prince (CEO) leads, guides, directs the organization into the future in accordance with the basic laws of the universe (according to the latest management thought). Happily, the prince is no longer thought to rule by divine right, though from the sluggishness of many boards to challenge their CEOs one might think the idea has lingered on. But he (and it is almost always a he) is nonetheless the prince, and his fiefdom (company) is a reflection of him, his goals, his desires, and—equally important—his personality.

Certainly, many current and recent corporate princes are very able men: Bob Galvin (Motorola), Jack Welch (GE), and David Kearns (Xerox) spring to mind. Many others, while undoubtedly able, have led their kingdoms to the brink of disaster and sometimes over this brink: Roger Smith (GM) can bear the standard for hundreds of other less well known princes.

Do we conclude that companies must do better at choosing princes? Probably not. As the organizational kingdoms grow and the environments in which they exist become more dynamic, the idea of the CEO as classic prince who, with a few trusted subordinates, can lead, direct, and guide them becomes more and more obsolete. No matter how intelligent, how well schooled, how ably seconded these individuals may be, reality continues to outrun their ability to deal with it.

This is where Charles Darwin and his discoveries come in. We need a new model of organization, one that moves organizational theory from the pre-Darwinian divinely ordered universe to one that accepts the reality of surprise, chance, and constant change. In short, we need a revolution in the way we look at organizations no less revolutionary than Darwin's view of biological evolution. And if we look closely at the thought of Darwin and his successors on biological evolution, we may find valuable ideas to help us accomplish this revolution.

This book shows how basic ideas derived from biological evolution can be applied to organizations, and applied in a way that makes organizations more flexible and able to respond successfully to their environments.

Make no mistake, though; this is no text on evolution. You will find virtually no details of evolution mentioned between its covers. Instead, it presents essential ideas and perspectives drawn from evolutionary theory that offer clear alternatives to the traditional ways of understanding organizations.

The Plan of the Book

If you've thought of evolution simply as "survival of the fittest," you may be surprised by many of the points in this book. Evolution has complex, subtle mechanisms that include but extend far beyond the well-known concepts of random mutation and natural selection. And many of these mechanisms apply, literally or suggestively, to the evolution of organizations. I describe these mechanisms and how they apply to organizations in a sequence that moves from familiar evolutionary ideas to those that are much less familiar. This is the basic outline:

Almost everyone knows that evolutionary change takes a very long time to produce useful change, and every change must begin with individual mutations. Because of this, useful change becomes an expensive, wasteful process. Thank heavens planned organizational change is different—or is it? Chapter 1 answers that question.

Both biologists and marketers use the concept of a niche. All biological survival occurs in a specific niche; so does organizational survival. But niches are dangerous. Specifically, the more fully an organism or organization adapts to a niche, the more vulnerable it is to new competitors, especially if the niche changes or vanishes. Chapter 2 explores the impact of niches and their relationship to organizational equilibrium and entropy—a relationship all too often overlooked.

The idea of a niche leads to another key idea: Both organisms and organizations thrive to the extent that their overall structure fits the requirements of their environments. The overall structure of an organization consists of its technology; its functions, processes, and organizational structure; its incentives; its competence; its culture; and the use it makes of information. Chapter 3 looks at the impact of the first four of these component systems.

Information is the key to both biological and organizational evolution. Organisms come into being from the information contained in their DNA; they survive by their ability to get and use information from their environments. What we call "organizational culture" resembles DNA; it preserves the form of the organization from generation to generation. But for the organization to survive it must get and assimilate information from its environment—a chancier and less effective process for organizations than most people believe. Chapter 4 examines the crucial function of information, both as culture and as what we generally refer to as "information."

Simple organisms, such as bacteria, respond rapidly to changes in their external environments. More complex organisms, such as humans and their organizations, respond both to their external environments and to the internal environments created by their more elaborate internal structures. In biology, the more complex an organism is, the more its evolution will be determined by its internal structure. So it is with organizations; the more complex their structures, the more their operations will be determined by internal events and relationships rather than by changes in their environments. Chapter 5 points out the crucial part played by internal structure in an organization's evolution—or extinction, as the case may be.

What we commonly call evolution is really *co*evolution. No organism evolves in a vacuum. Its survival depends on what other organisms in its environment are doing—particularly those organisms that are competitors, predators, or prey. Organizations operate similarly; organizational choices are meaningless apart from the choices made by competitors, customers, government bodies, and all other elements of their environments. Traditional organizational theory often gave this critical fact little or no attention. Chapter 6 looks closely at it.

Biological evolution is often depicted as a smooth process from simpler to more complex organisms. Organizational evolution too often seems equally smooth and predictable. If we look backward at either form of evolution, this seems true. But when we look forward, when we attempt to predict what will happen in the future, smoothness and predictability are nowhere to be found. The real truth of biological and organizational evolution is simple: The future can neither be controlled nor predicted. No one can predict from any one point in time what direction evolution will take. And no organization can predict how it will evolve. In fact, all too often organizations are unable to predict the final form or impact of their own innovations. Chapter 7 confronts these painful but important truths.

How can an organization survive, much less thrive, in so uncertain an environment? Scientists have discovered a phenomenon at work in evolution—and also at every other level of

existence: self-organization. Within the limits of their environments, all complex biological organisms, including all functioning humans, are self-organizing. In fact, *all* human organization
is ultimately self-organization. This idea runs directly counter to
the basic tenets of traditional organizational theory and practice.
But developing the self-organizing abilities of its component
units, down to the working level, may well be the only way that
organizations, like organisms, can survive. Chapter 8 analyzes
self-organization and suggests how organizations can use it to
their advantage.

What could have less to do with biological and organizational evolution than free enterprise? It antedated Darwin's theories by about a century, yet it takes on new life when viewed
within the context of evolution. Can an organization have internal free enterprise and compete successfully? It not only can,
it must. Chapter 9 explains why, for reasons that may surprise
you.

"Punctuated equilibrium" has become a new and contro-
versial theory of biological evolution. Biological organisms don't
evolve in smooth, continuous patterns as Darwin thought they
did. Instead, they remain stable for long periods of time, then
appear to evolve rapidly in a short time. The theory seems likely,
but not all evolutionary biologists accept it. On the other hand,
this theory offers the most cogent explanation available for how
and why organizations can stay in touch with their environments and change effectively. Chapter 10 ends the book by
looking at the theory and its very clear implications for organizations.

A Changed Worldview

Beneath every theory lies a view of the world. From the medieval
period to the nineteenth century the worldview of Western civilization was that of a static, well-ordered universe founded on
eternal, knowable principles. This worldview fit reality less and
less well as the years rolled by; the American and French revolu-
tions occurred some eighty years before Darwin wrote *Origin*

of Species. Nonetheless, that was the prevalent worldview until Darwin's work changed it.

How did it change? Darwin described a world in which:

1. All organisms live within a dynamic field of potentials. Change is constant and there is never just one path to the future.
2. The different potentials are always in tension with, often competing with, each other. Each promises a payoff, and each cuts the organisms off from other promising paths.
3. These tensions are resolved and evolution occurs through events (random mutations) occurring in an uncertain environment, and the results of these events cannot ever be adequately forecast.
4. Just as no one can forecast the results of these events, no one can effectively control them once they have occurred, because the results are created, moment by moment, from the interaction (coevolution) of all the players involved in the environment.
5. Consequently, the future is never fully contained in the present. Life exists and evolves through novel and unpredictable paths. The future remains unpredictable, both in theory and in fact.

Don't these five characteristics describe the competitive world of the late 1990s as well as the world of biological evolution? Don't they appear to describe this world far better than any theory based on unchanging management principles and rigid hierarchy? I think they do—but we need to make one change, a very important change.

People Make Choices

In the nonhuman world, change appears to occur without the involvement of direct choice. But human beings make choices, and these choices strongly influence their individual and organizational evolution. This doesn't mean that change happens the way that you and I and the CEO of Superior Worldwide Chemical intend it to. Very often, the most valuable part of change is the part that isn't predicted. But, on the human level, individual choices *always* affect both what change occurs and how it occurs.

Any number of scientists and "scientific" movements have declared that individual humans are no more than the products of their heredity, their environment, or immutable natural law (or all of them). Marx thought that the outcome of history was controlled by dialectical forces that individuals were powerless to control. Freud thought that most of us most of the time were the prisoners of our libidos. Many behaviorists believe that we are the sum of the responses we have made under the control of the stimuli we have encountered. In fact, it appears to be almost an article of scientific faith that free choice and human intent are illusory.

I specifically reject this. Human beings are in fact influenced by an endless sequence of external events. (They put my dog to sleep when I was six; I am amazed at how much of my subsequent life was unconsciously influenced by my reaction to that event.) But none of us are merely hostages to these events, either individually or in the aggregate. The events in our lives create both opportunities and limitations for each of us; they do not ultimately create or control us.

But that's not really why I reject the thesis that human behavior is determined by forces outside our control. My reason is a simple matter of observation: When individuals are treated as if they are autonomous beings with meaningful freedom of choice, they turn out better than if they are not. When individuals are not so treated, an interesting phenomenon emerges. The people who treat them as if they are determined, as less than free and autonomous human beings, see *themselves* as free and autonomous. In other words, almost everyone who believes that human action is determined believes, implicitly or explicitly, that it is the *other person* who is not free.

Individuals often cannot forecast the results of their actions; if this were not the case, life would be a bowl of week-old cherries and I wouldn't need to write this book. But individual actions are intentional. Each actor on the organizational stage always has the option to do something other than what he or she actually does. Because of that, no matter how suggestive

physical and biological evolution may be, the evolution of organizations is ultimately caused by the interaction of intentional
human beings. On that premise, this book is built. For organizations, human choice is the vital link between the world of potentials and the world of actuality.

From Theory to Practice

Theory is nice; at its best it's even exciting and enlivening. But
theory by itself never helped meet a payroll. So this book combines what I believe is solid theory with practice in two ways.
First, scattered through the chapters are sections headed *A Brief
Reality Check*. You can read this book without doing any of these
checks, but you can evaluate the theory far more realistically if
you take a few moments to do them. They will help you relate
the ideas to your own experience and give you a more realistic
perspective on both the ideas and your experience.

Second, many chapters end with concrete lessons for organizational practice drawn from the ideas presented in the chapter. These lessons will enable you to test the ideas in your own
organization. Only then will you know whether they will work
for you.

1

Open Your Pocketbook—Here Comes the Change

Successful change is very expensive in nature. Successful change is also very expensive for organizations.

The earth has existed for about four and a half billion years. It took four billion of these years for crustaceans—life-forms advanced enough to leave fossils—to appear. It then took another 497 million years for life to progress from hard-shelled marine creatures to human beings.

Let's reduce this to human scale. Picture a great evolutionary football game. If we condense the time from the appearance of crustaceans to the present to 60 minutes, the length of a professional football game, human beings get into the game with less than half a minute remaining. Then civilized humans get to play so short a time that the scoreboard clock shows 0 minutes and 0 seconds (actually 1/500th of a second) when we enter the game.

Why does it take so long? Because evolutionary change depends on random (or near-random) mutations. Remember Biology 101? A mutation is a difference between parents and child that the child can pass on to its offspring. If First Officer Spock's eldest son were to have ears that were rounded instead of pointed and if Spock, Jr.'s son had round ears, round ears would be a mutation. But unless round ears conferred some competitive advantage on him—such as fulfilling an ancient prophecy that the Great Leader of the People would arise with round ears—they would be an interesting but irrelevant mutation. They wouldn't lead anywhere.

How many mutations does it take to produce one that begins to create a new and competitive species? We know of no viable new species that has arisen during the whole of human history, which means that the billions upon billions of mutations that have occurred during the last few thousand years have failed to produce an improvement in even one species. Sooner or later, a series of mutations will result in a new species that survives. And over millions of years, thousands of other new species will come into being that compete successfully.

The point? Nature expends incredible amounts of resources to produce a few small but successful changes. What about organizations?

How Organizations Change

Compared with biological change, organizational change is incredibly fast and uses virtually no resources in the process. An organization can change in a millionth of the time it takes just one species to evolve slightly. In human terms, though, the change can and often does occur very, very slowly. And, in human terms, an organization can expend tremendous amounts of the resources available to it just to produce small lasting changes.

At first glance, organizational change seems to distinguish itself from biological change in two significant ways:

1. Biological change is based on random occurrences (mutations), while organizational change is planned. GE remains extremely successful because Jack Welch, its CEO, has a clear plan for the future of the organization and changes the organization in accordance with this plan.
2. Biological change occurs in one individual at a time, while organizational change occurs in large subunits or

large organizations. IBM as a whole is changing, not just a random computer assembler or statistical clerk.[1]

If these are valid distinctions, we should expect organizations to be quite effective at changing. But are appearances perhaps deceptive? Is organizational change actually quite expensive, even wasteful, and perhaps dangerous? Here are some of the facts and suspected facts about change in the late 1990s.

The core reality is this: Major change in organizations typically does not succeed. The data available on total quality management (TQM) and reengineering programs indicate that no more than a third of the planned changes achieve their goals. The very incomplete data on downsizing and "rightsizing" suggest that even fewer of these changes achieve their goals for more than a few months. Specifically, the data suggest that a company that downsizes without a major change in organization and culture will experience a short-term reduction in costs—which quickly shrinks or vanishes.

Depressing as they are, these results are more heartening than those reported by Alan Wilkins in his excellent book *Developing Corporate Character:*

> For the past seven years, I have gathered information on companies that have been attempting self-proclaimed "culture" change. . . . My sample now includes twenty-two organizations, both large and small; half of them are Fortune 500 size. They also represent organizations in several different industries. . . .
>
> Managers in at least sixteen of these twenty-two organizations would label their attempts at major change a failure. That is, they have not achieved their objectives, and in many cases their efforts have created serious cynicism among employees because the company was unable to change as promised. Two of the companies are not clearly a success or failure, while executives in the remaining four organizations feel they have mainly succeeded in making dramatic changes.[1]

(Just for the record, that constitutes a maximum success rate of less than 28 percent.)

The Chanciness of Change

Do you perhaps have a different impression? Do you think of GE or Xerox or Compaq as examples of successful change? In fact, they are. But these few highly publicized successes may be misleading.

1. Chrysler has become masterful at design but keeps tripping over poor quality. Ford succeeded with the Taurus but then turned in a so-so performance for the next few years, which included never quite correcting the abysmal quality of the Tempo. It was at least the mid-1990s before GM appeared to be finding the key. We are talking here about changes that took years, even (in GM's case) well over a decade. And we have no idea how successful any of the Big Three would be if such severe limitations were not placed on Japanese imports, and if the value of the dollar was not so historically low against the yen.

2. For perfectly understandable reasons, corporations not only downplay but, whenever possible, hide their failures. Nowhere is this more true than in the management information system (MIS) arena. How many major MIS changes have you read about that failed? Perhaps one or two? But anyone who reads between the lines of periodicals like *Information Week* gets a dramatically different view. Unknown billions of dollars are written off each year by American corporations in failed computer systems implementations that never surface. Yet no aspect of organizational life uses more careful and detailed planning methods than does the implementation of such systems.

3. Even when you read a "success" story, it probably has this characteristic: Its proponents report the "success" well before the results of the change are in. The business press bears a share of the blame for this, but it is simply one offender among many. Every year, dozens of associations hold conferences at which academics, consultants, managers, and other "change agents" report on their latest successes. Sadly, most of these successes have barely been implemented. For example, at a major conference on human resources management innovations in the mid-1990s, *not a single innovation described at the conference had*

been implemented for as long as a year! Then, three to five years later, when the real results of the change become apparent, no one is around to provide an objective, unbiased account of these results—or has any interest in doing so. In fact, a cynic might suspect that no one is available to report because most of these change agents are out installing new change programs in organizations where the "successes" of a few years before turned out to be duds.

4. While accurate figures on the results of change are all but impossible to come by, it is almost certain that the real cost of most change is seriously understated. Change has five different but related costs. Four of these are dollars, time, effort, and attention. (The next paragraph describes the fifth and most important cost.) Corporations reliably track highly visible dollar costs, which may include the dollar costs associated with observable drops in production. They seldom, if ever, capture the costs of the time taken by managers and workers who must implement the change or of the effort devoted to the change that was diverted from other activities. No organization, to my knowledge, has ever calculated the costs of the attention focused on the change effort that should have been directed elsewhere. And this leads to the final and most significant reason that change efforts are often not so successful as they seem.

5. Economists have talked for years of the *opportunity cost* of any decision. The opportunity cost is simple to state but difficult to measure in that it consists of the advantage lost by an organization because it spent time, money, effort, and attention on one goal rather than another. How does a company measure this? It cannot, as a general rule. The following statement, though, may suggest a general standard:

> Large organizations are talking more and more about the challenge of keeping ahead of competitors by generating new services for customers while simultaneously reducing costs, increasing productivity, enhancing quality and improving management effectiveness.[2]

Most organizations, most of the time, seem to start with "reducing costs." How many accounts do you remember reading of organizations that have solved the problem of "surplus employees" by increasing customer value (as reflected in market share, new markets, increased value to current customers, and so forth) instead of by axing workers? Yet beginning by generating new services for customers will almost always lead to the most productive and most successful forms of organizational change. For example, at one 1994 conference on reengineering—not a methodology known for its customer focus—virtually every speaker who presented a true success story made it clear that reengineering succeeded primarily because it helped the corporation focus more closely on the customer.

There are exceptions. Compaq Computers changed dramatically, changed quickly, and changed to provide value to its customers. The company built its reputation as a provider of relatively expensive, high-quality computers to corporations. To all appearances, it succeeded admirably at this. But the board of directors ousted Ron Canion, founder of the company, and installed Eckhard Pfeiffer as CEO. In about eighteen months, Pfeiffer completely redirected the company, and by the end of 1994 Compaq had become the world's number one maker of personal computers. If the company had simply stayed in its niche and concentrated on cutting costs, it could have claimed success. But think of how high the opportunity costs would have been, when compared to what the company actually accomplished.

In economic jargon, when an organization focuses its change efforts on increasing its value to its markets, it normally minimizes the opportunity costs of its actions. Conversely, when it attacks a subsidiary problem, no matter how successfully it does so, it raises its opportunity costs. An organization may not be able to measure its opportunity costs, but in the long run minimizing these costs counts for far more than simply minimizing operating costs.

A Brief Reality Check

The paragraphs you've just read are accurate, but safe. They concern other organizations, other people, other changes. But what about your own organization, its people, and its changes? Why not take a moment to look at your organization and the success of its changes?

Find a piece of letter-size or larger paper and a pen or pencil. Relax in your chair and make a list down the left side of the paper of the major planned changes your organization has initiated over the last ten years (or less, if you've not been with it for ten years). Include every planned change, whether it was designed to improve morale, increase productivity, increase customer service, reduce cycle time, or whatever. Take your time; you want to ensure that you catch each and every change in your imaginative net.

Now that you have identified all the changes, remind yourself of the results of each change program and grade each of these results. Here are the grades you might use:

A　　The change was *completely successful*. It produced substantially all the benefits its proponents had claimed for it, and one of the benefits it produced was greater value to the company's customers (including successfully finding new customers and/or new markets).

B　　The change was *partially successful*. It produced enough benefits to clearly outweigh the costs (dollars, time, effort, and attention) of implementing it.

?　　The change is too *new* to tell whether it will be successful or not.

F　　The change *failed*. It did not deliver enough of its promised benefits to be worth the effort and was abandoned. If this was the case, you can assume that the change was at least to some extent counterproductive. In other words, the company would have been better off if it had not tried the change.

I　　The change is *incomplete*. It is clearly not successful, but it has not been abandoned. In short, it is one of the *walking wounded:* It continues to absorb resources and drain attention away from other projects without any promise of delivering results. In many ways, this result harms the company more than any other.

A company that changed effectively would have one or two major change programs going plus a few minor ones, and each change would be graded at least a *B*. Companies at the other end of the scale probably tried more major and minor changes but get mainly *F*s and *I*s for their efforts.

What grades would your company get? For many, many companies, at least half their grades would be *F*s and *I*s. And remember, every failed or walking-wounded change represents a significant cost to the company, a cost for which it received no return or even a negative return.

Perhaps companies don't change all that quickly and effectively after all. Could it be that, like evolutionary change, planned organizational change expends large amounts of resources to produce only a few successful changes? We will never have all the data we need to answer this question once and for all. But we have some compelling reasons for thinking the answer is yes.

The Pitfalls of Planned Change

Data on currently fashionable changes and their success rates are notoriously hard to come by. But we can get some hints if we look at strategic planning, one of the most basic and highly articulated forms of planned change. Like current planned change programs, strategic planning looks five to ten years into the future (sometimes even further) and determines how the organization should proceed. The task of strategic change, however, is considerably easier than that of cultural change; it seldom requires the organization to do other than move in a more-or-less straight line from its current situation to a future one. So, if significant organizational change holds the prospect of success, strategic planning should have been a resounding success.

Has it been this success? Hardly. One of the first shots fired at strategic planning was launched by Kenichi Ohmae. In his 1983 book, *The Mind of the Strategist,* he said:

> We have all witnessed the heyday of the giant enterprise, the days when it seemed that big U.S. companies, and later big European companies, could really end up controlling the whole world. Something happened to prevent it. There has been a marked decline in the ability of large corporations to cope with the changes that confront them. In these companies, brains and muscles were separated, destroying the entire body's coordination. On one hand there were the brains; on the other there was the muscle—the people of the enterprise. They were there to make the plan a reality, to carry out the brain's instructions. . . .
>
> In effect, most large U.S. corporations are run like the Soviet economy. Many are centrally planned for three to five years, with their managers' actions spelled out in impressive detail for both normal and contingency conditions. During the ongoing implementation process, each manager is "monitored" on how accurately he has been adhering to the agreed objectives.
>
> Long study of communist and socialist regimes has convinced many observers that detailed long-range planning coupled with tight control from the center is a remarkably effective way of killing creativity and entrepreneurship at the extremities of the organization.[3]

Ohmae's final comment is particularly telling, because innovation—successful change—typically occurs "at the extremities of the organization."

Mr. Ohmae goes on to compare American top-down planning with the Japanese method of solving problems, in which "only active and alert organization members, working as an integrated team, can properly address and resolve them."[4] Numerous writers in the late 1980s and early 1990s advocated moving closer to the Japanese model. Unfortunately, between 1983 and the 1990s, most Japanese corporations concluded that their traditional "bottom-up" method of planning by consensus was as inadequate for today's competitive environment as American strategic planning was and began to explore other methods.

Without question, the most highly publicized *successful* use of strategic planning was Shell Oil's use, beginning in the 1970s, of "scenario planning," in which not one but several futures were postulated and explored. The method succeeded at least once; it prepared Shell to deal with the oil crisis of the 1970s more effectively than did most of its competitors. Note, however, that it represents a significant step away from conventional planning in that it attempts to prepare the corporation to deal with multiple futures. It also requires considerably more imagination and effort on the part of the planners. Most important, despite its apparent advantages, it has not registered any equivalent subsequent successes.

Recently, Henry Mintzberg sounded what may be long-range strategic planning's death knell in *The Rise and Fall of Strategic Planning*, one whole chapter of which is devoted to "Fundamental Fallacies of Strategic Planning." Some of Mintzberg's criticisms are directed at planning per se and apply only marginally here. Others are directly relevant. One in particular, however, is as telling for organizational change in general as it is for strategic planning. The simple truth is this: No one's forecasts turn out to be very reliable.[5]

At first glance, organizational change, unlike strategic planning, appears not to require significant forecasting on the part of the corporation. But stop and think a moment. In an organization of any size, even a relatively modest change takes one to three years to implement successfully. A "transformational" or "cultural" change may require a decade or more. (Remember, GM started to change early in the 1980s and appeared to be turning the corner only in the mid-to-late 1990s.) When the organization plans the change, it either assumes that the environment around the change will remain constant or that it can predict the significant changes in the environment. Neither of these assumptions holds up.

Let me provide an example about which I have some personal knowledge. A federal agency decided to develop leadership training for its executives and managers. Doing things the right way, it began by surveying executives and managers at all levels to identify the competencies that would be needed for leadership *three to five years into the future.* It then developed the training. By the time the training was ready to deliver, however, the actual leadership skills needed in the agency had changed so significantly that the training had to be shelved.

The rate of change in today's environment hardly appears to be slowing down. AT&T's Universal Card Services won the Baldrige in 1992—and immediately began to reengineer itself. Most CEOs in organizations that have changed successfully see no end to the changes. Early technology adopters, like Baxter, are perhaps upgrading their technological base even more rapidly than the companies that are attempting to catch up with them.

Some of the changes in the environment can be predicted: More homes will have computers (probably); air travel to and from vacation areas will rise (probably); the Balkan situation will remain unstable (almost certainly). But what will be the impact on home computers and television sets of dramatically increasing communication speeds? Will the instability of the Balkans spread beyond that area, and if it does, what will its impact be? What types of toys will be most popular three years from now? Not only do we not know the answers to these questions, but we do not even know whether they are the right questions to ask.

Which brings us to the heart of the matter: No organization that initiates long-range change today can have any real assurance that the change will be relevant in two, much less five, years. Clearly, the longer the change requires, the less able the organization will be in predicting the competitive situation at the end of the change. So time and the unpredictability of the future are major causes of (as an annual report might put it) less-than-successful change. In short, an organization that changes to reach a defined target more than a year or two into the future is aiming at a target that is both moving and rapidly changing.

Tom Peters summarized the matter in this sentence: "Unintended consequences and secondary effects of most actions far outnumber intended and first-order effects."[6]

Or, as Yogi Berra said, "the future ain't what it used to be." Ever.

One Size Never Fits All

As though the unpredictability of the future weren't enough, company after company sets itself up for failure in its change efforts. How? By determining the change it needs to make from the limited menu of currently popular changes available at any given time. TQM was the change program of choice in the 1980s. It was joined by self-managing work teams, reengineering, and "rightsizing" at the beginning of the 1990s. By the mid-1990s, TQM had generally lost its luster; the merits of self-managing teams were beginning to be debated; "rightsizing" continued to thrive without conclusive data on its success; and business process reengineering had become largely a synonym for downsizing.

We all know this, yet companies continue to limit their change strategies to the most popular choices. Why? One reason is the sheer cost of information. It takes time and effort to find out the full range of available alternatives and then select the most promising one. It seems to require less time, money, and effort to choose among those that appear to be succeeding at other companies—particularly if the CEO of one or more of these companies is well known and well respected. Why not go with success?

Another reason, a well-documented one, is that American executives aren't oriented toward planning and analysis. Strategic planning failed in part because companies relegated it to its own department, where it became increasingly irrelevant to the real life and problems of the company. The pressures of Wall Street for short-term results play some part in this; the results that matter are the results that can be produced in a matter of months, which leaves no time for planning and analysis. But most individuals who become executives do so because they've demonstrated that they are "action" people. In fact, many take pride in the fact that they aren't analysts, that they won't tolerate "analysis paralysis." As they see it, making a quick search, picking an available program, and going with it beats wasting time on data collection and analysis every time.

The sheer pace of change at the end of the twentieth century is yet another reason. We've already seen that any company that selects a change program based on its view of the situation three to five years into the future is treading on ice that gets thinner as each day passes. Why devote months to analyzing available change strategies when the problem may have changed shape by the time the strategy is selected?

Even if you could solve all these problems, the basic problem would remain. As the introduction stressed, life at any given moment presents a number of potential courses of action, and the results of each course are inherently uncertain. Actions that appear safe may promise unacceptably low returns, while those with high payoffs may entail unacceptably high risks. For instance, business process reengineering on a large scale involves high risk, while the results of business process reengineering on a small scale seldom justify the effort.

None of this supports a "shoot first, ask questions later" approach to organizational change. The value of effective up-front investigation and analysis has been demonstrated time and again; the ability to come up with a rich range of alternatives remains the best single predictor of success. But organizations can come up with and choose from this range of alternatives in today's environment only when information can be found, processed, and used quickly and effectively. How they can do this forms the substance of this book.

The Illusion of "Organizational" Change

We thought that organizational change might be comparatively less wasteful than biological change because it was planned. The facts don't bear this out. But we had a second reason for thinking it might be less wasteful: Biological change occurs in one individual at a time, whereas organizational change occurs in large subunits or large organizations as a whole. This sounds commonsensical; perhaps it contains the solution to our problem of successful change. Unfortunately, this assumption falls apart as completely as did the first assumption. The simple fact is this:

Only individuals can decide to change, and only individuals can actually change.

This certainly seems to contradict our everyday experience. After all, we read that IBM must change, that Sears is changing, or that Kmart seems unable to change successfully. True, but in each of these cases a legal fiction—that a corporation is a single entity—hides the truth from us. What we call organizational change is no more or less than the sum total of changes decided upon and made by the individuals who comprise that organization.

Xerox was one of the clear success stories of the 1980s. To all appearances, the corporation really did change. But what about the individual who represents Xerox to you, the one who sells you your copier or services it? If that individual continues to act the same, has Xerox changed? Wait a minute. Their processes changed, and this happened independently of individual choices, didn't it? Not really. Someone proposed what the new processes should be, others commented on them and tried to alter them to fit their own needs, and yet others have to apply them—or choose not to. And this constitutes just a minute fragment of what a giant global organization is. Multiply this fragment by thousands and you have tens of thousands of individuals making their individual decisions about how and whether to change.

But don't individuals affect each other? Don't teams and work groups make joint decisions? Yes. Close-knit groups have significant influence on the decisions of their members. Yet even then, only individuals can make decisions, and individuals often work to sabotage a group decision that they supposedly participated in making. Moreover, this kind of strong influence is limited to small groups. The copier repairer who comes when you call may reflect the "culture" of the small group of repairers in his immediate office, but the thoughts and actions of Xerox's CEO might as well be occurring on Mars. For him to be influenced by the CEO—currently Paul Allaire—dozens, if not hundreds, of others must first be influenced. As you might guess, all this takes time. If you think I have overstated my case, read *Prophets in the Dark,* the joint account by David Kearns, CEO of Xerox at the time, and David Nadler, his primary consultant, of the change at Xerox.

The fact that only individuals can change, and that influencing them to change requires a great deal of time and effort, makes planned change uncertain on at least two scores:

1. Even a relatively simple change takes time, since hundreds, thousands, or even tens of thousands of individuals must decide to make individual changes in consonance with the change planned for the organization. We have already seen that the sheer passage of time militates against effective change, because the more time that passes the more the environment changes in unpredictable ways.

2. No individual ever decides to change in exactly the way the organization expects. Even with the best intent, she will understand incompletely just what she should do. Even with the best intent, she will slant the change in the direction of her own goals and desires. And without the best intent, she will distort, conceal, and even lie to avoid some or all of the desired change. Then, to cover this, she and her colleagues will submit reports that exaggerate the change that has actually occurred. Don't take this as a cynical overstatement. A primary survival skill in organizations has always been the ability to generate reports that demonstrate one's commitment to the current program without making significant changes at any point. If you are a CEO with more than three levels between yourself and the people who actually get the work done, I trust that you routinely take these kinds of reports with a boulder or so of salt.

Change Is Expensive: The Lessons

What useful conclusions can you draw from our beginning excursion into evolutionary ideas? Here are three nominations:

1. If you and your organization get into a situation where "cultural" or "transformational" changes are required, well,

you're in deep trouble indeed. Go ahead; bite the bullet. Do whatever changing you must. But instead of rejoicing in cultural change, link the new technologies, processes, and behaviors you want as tightly as possible to the existing values and operations of the organization. Don't make grand and glorious pronouncements; don't promulgate equally glorious visions or grand mission statements. Decide where you need to go, be as specific as possible about how you plan to get there, *provide clear incentives for individuals to change as you want them to change,* and then do it.

2. Look at *change* for a moment from an evolutionary perspective. Visualize, if you will, five different species competing for dominance in a niche. One species begins by being faster of foot than its competitors. Each of the other species makes the identical response: It attempts to improve its own speed to catch up with and then keep up with the first species. What do you think of that as a competitive strategy? How successful are the competing species apt to be? Not very. But how does this differ from corporate competition based on the management fad of the moment—whether it's TQM, "rightsizing," empowered teams, or whatever? Not very much, right? If the best you can do is to adopt a change strategy that apes that of your competitors, or that they are currently adopting, where are you likely to get? Perhaps by running at top speed you can keep from falling further behind.

3. Whatever you believe about your ability to change your organization, remember this key point: All change is individual change. All the talking, preaching, and jargoning in the world won't alter that. Individuals change if, and only if, they have a clear reason to change, and that covers the subject. When the smoke clears, the success of any organizational change rests on the payoff that each individual in the organization sees for the change—coupled with the strength of his or her belief that the change will actually occur. If you intend to produce significant change, concentrate on this point. Why would employees want to do what you want them to do? Only when you have a clear answer to this question can you have any assurance that the change you want is the change that will happen. On the subject

of motivation, the threat "Either change or you'll lose your job" has not proved dramatically successful. If you must use it, at least base it on something other than your simple assertion. Open the company's books and explain what they mean. Use relevant marketing data. Get executives out talking to workers and being honest with them. But don't expect anyone simply to take your word for it.

Alternatively, read on. You'll find better change strategies than just patching up last year's change model.

2

A Niche in Time Saves—or Does It?

Evolutionary success breeds sometime success and frequent failure. So does organizational success.

One of the truisms in biological evolution is this: Every species that succeeds does so in a specific niche. Some species occupy niches that are small indeed. Flowerflies, for example, exist by feeding only on aphids; one small wasp provokes an insect-eating ant lion into seizing it so it can lay its eggs inside the ant lion; another fly, potentially more useful to human beings, injects an egg into a fire ant that turns into a maggot and decapitates the ant.

Other species operate in far more widespread niches; every high school biology student knows that paramecia make their homes in pools of water over most of the world, and whales range over most of the ocean system. Human beings have adapted to virtually every land environment that exists. We can be found from the burning sands of the Sahara to the high plains of the Himalayas, from the monsoons and penetrating heat of the tropics to the frozen wastelands of the Arctic Circle.

Over evolutionary time, however, most organisms that ever existed have become extinct. Species vanish from the earth regularly, perhaps several thousand a year. Of the 912 species of animals and plants listed under the federal Endangered Species Act, eight became extinct within the first twenty-one years. At times, mass extinctions occur. The most extensive of all extinctions occurred at the end of the Permian age, some 245 million years ago, when 95 percent of the species that existed departed the evolutionary stage forever.

Why do species vanish from evolutionary history? Most of them, and we know little or nothing about them, perish because they fail to compete successfully in the only niches available to them. Some other species is already exploiting the niche more effectively. More fortunate species succeed in their niche for millions of years, but then become extinct because another creature that proves to be more successful in that niche moves in. Yet others, individually or in mass, vanish because their niche changes or vanishes and they cannot succeed outside the niche. This may happen in the next century, for instance, if the ocean reefs in several parts of the world continue to be eaten away; if they vanish, many of the organisms that inhabit them will also vanish.

Evolution has few truly lasting successes. And most of these successes are relatively simple organisms, because as organisms become more complex, extended survival becomes more precarious. In other words, in the evolutionary arena success is fleeting and no amount of current success guarantees future success. Could it be that this applies as well to organizations?

The Attraction of Niches

Both organisms and organizations find comfort in a good niche. One assumes that a paramecium, if asked, would express deep satisfaction with its pool of muddy water. Certainly the Big Three car companies were satisfied with their dominance of the American automobile market in the 1970s, just as IBM was with its dominance of mainframe computers from the 1960s through the 1980s. And Japanese companies are fighting furiously to protect their domestic niches from invasions from abroad, just as European automakers fight equally furiously to protect their niches against the Japanese.

A young organization, attempting to find its niche, move into it, and then enlarge it, often lives with continual change. As it expands, it must increase the scope of its operations—find new sales channels, develop more sophisticated internal management methods, articulate itself into more and more specialized internal functions. These form part of the normal growing pains of an expending organization; every company that experiences normal growth also experiences these pains.

Companies do not simply grow, however. Consciously or unconsciously, each one must select a niche in which to compete. Competitive niches have been defined in various ways by various authors. Michael Treacy and Fred Wiersema in their book *The Discipline of Market Leaders* define a three-niche structure, which can be broken down in this way:

- A company may compete by practicing *operational excellence*. It offers middle-of-the-market products at the best price with the least inconvenience to customers. Most home electronics manufacturers follow this strategy, as do most of the mass retailers who sell their products.
- A company may compete by pursuing *product leadership*. It offers products that push performance boundaries by continuing to innovate year after year. 3M has established its reputation by competing in this niche; so have Intel and a number of highly specialized medical equipment firms.
- Finally, a company may compete by exercising *customer intimacy*, selecting a small, well-defined niche in which it knows the needs of its customers intimately and makes responsiveness to these needs its primary competitive weapon. For example, hundreds of companies, most very small, provide expert training and consulting in such areas as OSHA and EPA compliance or nuclear waste disposal to a limited clientele.[1]

When an organization selects a basic strategy, it launches itself in a particular niche and attempts to expand in this niche. The niche may be very large, as is the worldwide niche for ink jet and laser printers that Hewlett-Packard currently dominates. Or it may be the business equivalent of the flowerfly, such as the hundreds of niches occupied by companies that exist to provide specialized products to automotive manufacturers.

Companies typically begin by serving either a small niche

or a small portion of a larger niche. If the company succeeds, it begins to fill as much of the niche as its competitive situation permits. Then it faces the critical decision: What now?

In general, a company that has expanded to the limits of its niche evolves in one of four ways:

1. It ceases evolving and grows only as rapidly as its niche expands, remaining content in its initial niche. Companies that succeed at this seldom make good copy for management journals and the business press, but thousands of companies find it a fully viable option. Many management consultancies composed of one to a dozen partners remain happily in their initial specialized niches. Despite its wide variety of products, IBM remained rooted in its initial niche, mainframe computers, until competitive conditions in the 1990s made the strategy obsolete. (At least, that's the common wisdom. As 1995 began, IBM's profit margin on mainframes was down, but it was moving them out the door as fast as it could make them.)

2. It attempts to evolve by enlarging its original niche. It accomplishes this by finding new products or services to sell to existing customers or by finding new customers in closely related fields for its existing products and services. Orvis, a catalogue merchandiser, has expanded its line from fly-fishing equipment to a greater variety of sporting equipment to sports clothes and travel accessories. The Oreck Company, a manufacturer of industrial vacuum cleaners, expanded its niche by selling the same products through limited channels to homeowners.

3. It attempts to evolve by diversifying and expanding into new niches while still occupying its original niche. Compaq Computer achieved its initial success by selling very high quality computers to corporate accounts. Then, deciding that the market was changing rapidly, it moved dramatically outside its original niche and began selling low-cost personal computers to individuals and businesses through a variety of channels. (It also began selling printers for these computers, but that turned out not to be a success story.)

4. It attempts to evolve by leaving its initial niche altogether and moving into a different niche well outside its original one.

International Harvester first diversified from farm machinery into trucks, then sold its farm machinery business to concentrate entirely on this new niche. And who remembers that the FMC corporation, manufacturer of a wide variety of products, was once the Food Machinery Corporation?

Each niche, and each way of expanding from a niche, has its advantages and disadvantages. Each offers potential advantages and cuts off other advantages. Depending on the mood of the times, "good management practice" may favor one or the other. GM, Ford, and Chrysler learned painfully to "stick to their knitting." IT&T, by contrast, continues to operate with relative success in unrelated niches. We can leave these decisions up to the currently reigning management gurus. Instead, as you might expect from a book on organizational evolution, we want to look at the implications of the whole idea of niches on the evolution (successful change) of organizations.

Niches and Successful Organizational Change

We've already seen several basic pitfalls of planned organizational change: The future is unpredictable; change efforts are often selected only from among currently popular programs; and "organizational" change can never be more than the sum of decisions made by the individuals who compose it. Now, using the relationship between organizations and niches, we can get an even clearer picture of why so much organizational change fails.

First of all, different companies occupy very different kinds of niches. A planned change may make a company producing sufficient-quality products at low prices more successful in its niche. This same change would probably be irrelevant (and therefore harmful) to a similar company whose niche was an indepth understanding of its customers—and could be positively disastrous to a cutting-edge, innovative company. For instance, total quality management (TQM) was developed as a way of focusing organizational attention on identifying and producing routine products in a manufacturing environment. When properly applied in that environment, it can produce major improvements throughout a company. On the other hand, I have been trying for a decade to find a successful application of TQM principles to a knowledge-work environment, and I haven't found one yet.

Second, companies at different stages in their niches require very different kinds of changes. To illustrate this, consider reengineering. A company growing rapidly within its niche will always outgrow its original structure and processes. It will normally profit from reengineering several core processes, such as order fulfillment. However, no amount of reengineering will substitute for a complete revision of its organizational, managerial, and financial structure. For instance, a rapidly growing company can easily find itself short of cash—even if its internal processes are wonderful.

The fact is that TQM, reengineering, and the currently fashionable rightsizing were designed primarily for companies in relatively stable niches whose competitive positions were being threatened or who wanted to expand within their niches. Rightsizing makes sense only if the walls of the niche are high, thick, and barbed; otherwise, various other strategies to enhance revenue would make far more sense (and cause far less pain). What would have happened, for instance, if Chrysler had simply decided to rightsize instead of developing and marketing the minivan—the cash cow that fueled Chrysler's subsequent improvements, the ones that enabled it to make more money per car in the mid-1990s than any other automotive manufacturer in the world?

Third, no general strategies for change exist that will fit even similar companies in similar niches at similar stages in their competitive history. If some way existed (which it doesn't) to say that Company B is now at the same point that Company A was at six months ago, Company B would still not know what change to make. Company A's strategy may have been preemptive; no other firm can now adopt it successfully. The strategy may be failing, so Company B should avoid it like the plague. And even if it's available as a strategy, the sheer passage of six months may dictate an entirely different approach.

This makes the lemming mentality toward change described in Chapter 1 doubly dangerous. When a company concludes that it should get a reengineering program going at once *because* everyone else is doing reengineering, it sets itself up for costly (and often demoralizing) failure. The catchphrase "survival of the fittest" works better as polemic or propaganda than as science, but no one has ever seriously advocated "survival of the copycats" as an effective strategy.

I have often thought that if I were the CEO of a Fortune 500 company, I would put a member of my staff in charge of identifying all rising fads. As soon as a fad began to surface clearly, I'd set up a paper organization to implement the program in my company, head it with an extremely articulate executive, dress it up with my vision and mission statements and noble goals—and then make every major business publication aware of my dedication to the program. Having created that facade, in hopes that my competitors would jump on the same bandwagon, I would then focus sharply on where my real business opportunities lay and quietly put my horsepower there. But if I've thought of this, is it possible that some CEOs here or there may have had the same thought—and acted on it?

Finally, no company, whatever its circumstances, can be certain what its competitors will do. Even in very stable niches, a company may introduce an unexpected significant change. "Big Steel" knew who its competitors were and understood the terms of competition. It ignored minimills—until they began to seize significant market share. But most global niches aren't stable. Personal computers and their peripherals are the current paradigm of constant change, but this may well be overshadowed by the incredible changes occurring in communications.

The Entropic Organization

The idea of niches has one more lesson to teach before we move on. Organizations don't just occupy and succeed in niches. They also bloat and die in them. And two reasons for this, while present in biological evolution, transcend it. Organizations that succeed in their niches fall victim to the interaction between equilibrium and entropy. All systems try to move toward equilibrium, and all closed systems fall victim to entropy. Therein hangs an important tale.

Every stable living system tries to move to the condition that requires the least energy to maintain itself. This is its *equilibrium* state. (If you are familiar with chaos theory, you know the concept of complex, unstable systems in conditions far from equilibrium. Later parts of the book will deal with applications of chaos theory and specifically with complex adaptive systems. For now, however, we need to continue exploring systems that are seeking to operate at or near their equilibrium.)

What does equilibrium mean in organizational terms? Consider these examples:

- Any process requires some thought to execute. For an organization to serve its customers, it must be able to determine their needs and then translate these needs into products and/or services. The harder the organization has to think about the process of doing so, the more attention it must devote to it—and the less the time, energy, and money it has available for other processes. So the organization routinizes this process as quickly and fully as possible. Then, instead of having to hire marketing and product-development geniuses, it can hire ordinary marketers and product developers and teach them its process.

- All decisions require information, and information is costly. A company that wants to enter a new market must gather information about current competitors, cost of entry, possible future competitors, cost of leaving the market, and dozens of other factors. It must spend time, attention, effort, and money gathering this information. Consequently, because it operates in a risky world, it will tend over time to concentrate its effort on areas where it requires the smallest amount of new information. As part of this effort, it will tend to lodge the responsibility for getting the information in one or a few departments and will ignore information that might be available through "unauthorized" channels.

- Organizations operate internally through a web of relationships. Some of these relationships are clearly defined, like manager-subordinate, team leader-team member. More of them are defined fuzzily (one department head to another) or not defined at all (the friendship among three key secretaries). Some of these relationships work well for the organization; others don't. The head of manufacturing scarcely talks with the head of product design, so their subordinates must find a way to coordinate the two organizations. The head of sales is friends with the head of marketing, so she agrees to consider a change in the commission system that would pay for calls made in addition to sales made, even though her sales managers strongly oppose it. The VIP for finance is an alcoholic and no one deals directly with him unless forced to do so. Individuals throughout the organization know about all these problems, but the payoff from trying to change them never seems quite worth the effort (and risk). So the organization settles into an uneasy equilibrium that accepts all its problems as givens.

We've already seen that when an organization has identified its niche and filled it to the limits of its ability, it must choose whether simply to remain in the niche or to expand beyond it. Either is a live option for most companies, with its own set of promises and risks.

When an organization remains within a clearly defined (or perhaps even a not-so-clearly-defined) niche, it will move toward its equilibrium state. It may continue to compete within that niche, it may continue to develop new products or services. But to the extent it knows and serves a set niche, it will refine all its processes and activities to serve that niche with the least amount of effort. The more that its position is protected within the niche, the more this will be true.

The closer a company is to equilibrium within its present niche, the more it falls into the arms of equilibrium's traveling companion, *entropy*. And the more at home the organization is in its niche, the more it controls its markets, and the more constant a companion entropy becomes.

Entropy expresses one of the fundamental laws of the universe. Technically, entropy means the irreversible process by which heat flows from warmer areas to colder ones. The sun radiates heat to the universe surrounding it; it will keep doing so until its temperature is ultimately identical to that of its environment. The universe, at the macroscopic level, is moving unstoppably from order to disorder, from patterned processes to pure random ones.

Unfortunately, real-world entropy isn't limited to heat. In human affairs, particularly in organizations, entropy describes a basic tendency of systems to "run down." As organizations move toward equilibrium in a stable environment, processes and relationships become less and less efficient and effective. If we take the three examples of equilibrium-seeking from earlier in this section, this is how entropy might show itself:

- An organization attempts to routinize processes for identifying customer needs and then translate these needs into products and/or services. Time passes and times change, but these processes fail to change with them. The organization retains processes that once worked but no longer do so—and adds to them a new layer in its attempts to respond to current conditions. "That's the way it's done around here" becomes the watchword. Everything begins to take longer than it should, but the organization is protected, so no one really notices—or perhaps no one really cares. We associate this "hardening of the internal arteries" with government bureaucracies, and life would be far simpler if they indeed had a monopoly on it. Unfortunately, whenever *any* organization is protected from serious challenge from without, it will try to move toward equilibrium and entropy—and its public or private status matters as little as the color of the chairs in the executive dining room.

- An organization near equilibrium will tend over time to concentrate its efforts to secure information in areas where it requires the smallest amount of new information. It will accomplish this in part by limiting the intake of information to a small number of subordinate departments (marketing, public relations, perhaps R&D). These departments will "see" only the information they are chartered to see, and will put the appropriate organizational spin on this information. As the internally available information becomes more and more homogeneous, it captures less and less of external reality. Not surprisingly, homogeneity characterizes the effects of entropy; the universe will die a heat death because the heat in the universe will be so uniformly distributed that it will no longer support order of any kind. Organizations don't die heat deaths. In a very real sense, however, as an organization slips into entropy it dies an "information death."

▪ When an organization operates without strong external pressures, it concentrates more and more of its attention on its internal relationships. Because the heads of manufacturing and product design no longer have to focus sharply on external competitors, they can devote more time to their internal feud. Because of the same lack of competitive pressure, the head of marketing never brings up the changes that he believes his friend, the head of sales, ought to make. And no one any longer expects anything from the alcoholic head of finance.

The more an organization succeeds in its niche, the more quickly it falls victim to these entropic forces. It's quite fashionable to criticize companies that get caught when niches change or new competitors invade existing niches. The railroads failed to see beyond their existing niche and thus lost markets to the newer trucking industry. IBM failed to see the potential two decades ago in minicomputers, allowing Digital Equipment Corporation to become a major player in that market. Then Digital fell victim to the same niche-boundedness: Kenneth H. Olsen, the founder of Digital, concluded that "everyone will have [a personal computer]—tucked away in the closet" and ignored this major new market.[2] Most of the Japanese electronics giants, held up until recently as models of competitive success, are falling behind in several key digital technologies, most significantly in software. An entire industry, fabulously successful, is struggling to move beyond the niche in which its success occurred.

If we understand the power of the double whammy of equilibrium-seeking and entropy on a successful organization or industry, however, we ought not to wonder at a company that gets caught in its niche when the environment changes; rather, we should marvel at the few companies that don't. And we ought to look long and hard for the measures that organizations can take to avoid falling victim to these twin pressures.

The Real World of Organizations

The Introduction presented a short list of the characteristics of reality, a list that describes the world both of individuals and of organizations. While we would—or at least should—accept the list as common sense, it owes its foundation to the work of Charles Darwin. It might help to recapitulate some of the very specific applications of these ideas:

- Both organisms and organizations operate in a dynamic field of potentials. There is never just one path to the future. A company that has expanded fully within its niche will find promise in remaining within that niche, growing beyond it, expanding it, or even leaving it.
- The different potentials are always in tension with one another. Each promises a payoff, and each cuts the individual or company off from other payoffs. You can have a lot, but you can't have it all. In other words, a company may stick to its knitting or diversify; it cannot do both.
- These tensions can be resolved only by choices, choices made in an environment that is, at best, difficult to forecast. No divine law guarantees that one choice or set of choices will succeed. An organization that decides to remain in its niche runs the risk of entropy and obsolescence when its niche changes. An organization that decides to diversify runs the risk of fragmentation.
- No organization can control the results of the choices it makes, because reality is created moment by moment from the interaction of the choices made by all players involved in the environment. An organization's success at diversifying out of its niche will result from the decisions made by its members, by actual or potential competitors and their members, and probably by the decisions of dozens or thousands of individuals not visible at the time of the decision.
- The future of an organization is never simply contained in the present. An organization typically attempts to avoid the tensions and risks by finding and defending a niche. There, it may fall victim to the effects of entropy; a new competitor may

appear; an existing competitor may become more aggressive; or the niche may change or even vanish. No one can forecast which of these scenarios will be played out, particularly over several years or decades.

Niches: The Lessons

There are three major lessons that can be drawn from a study of niches.

1. *Companies that dominate their niches move toward equilibrium and in doing so fall victim to entropy.* They also fall victim to another, very human characteristic: arrogance. This constitutes an invitation that competitors and potential competitors just can't refuse. No one has summarized the situation better than Paul Ingrassia and Joseph B. White in their book *Comeback: The Fall & Rise of the American Automobile Industry:*

> The key to staying ahead in global competition is to understand that the battle is never really over. It is impossible to predict the winners and losers of tomorrow.
>
> In fact, today's winners tend to become tomorrow's losers, and vice versa. It's harder to stay on top than to get on top.[3]

Take stock of your own organization. Is it safely ensconced in its niche, protected from serious competition? Is it clearly superior to its competitors? Do profits—or, for that matter, congressional victories—come easy? Start worrying. It's harder to stay on top than to get on top.

2. *In order to fill a niche and reduce the danger of entropy and arrogance, you first have to define the niche.* Those flowerflies that exist by feeding only on aphids know their niche. So do the flies that inject their eggs into fire ants that decapitate the ant. That's no surprise. In nature, few if any creatures are confused about their niches; they have no real choice. But organizations do have

choices—and all niches are not created equal. You may like the breakdown that Treacy and Wiersema use, in which case you concentrate on operational excellence or product leadership or customer intimacy. You may prefer a different breakdown. Fine, use it. Just be clear as to what your market is, how you serve it, and what your competitive advantage is. "We intend to be the best provider of widgets in the world" looks great on a wall, but if you haven't a precise idea of your current market, product, and competitive advantage, any breakdown is just so much decoration.

3. *If you must adopt a traditional change program, be very, very sure you know what your niche is and how your company competes in it.* My preference should be obvious: Always attempt to change in ways that will increase revenue by increasing the value the organization provides its customers. But this is no more a one-size-fits-all prescription than any other. Your pressing problem may be to restructure the management of the organization or to develop a new cost-accounting system or even to do serious reengineering. Whatever the problem is, make sure that you adopt the change program that addresses this problem. And, for heaven's sake (and the sake of your customers, workers, suppliers, and stockholders), don't assume that because a particular change method is popular in your industry, or among your friends, it fills the bill.

3

What Makes Up an Organization?

The more complex an organism becomes, the more its internal structure will determine its evolution. The more complex your organization becomes, the more its internal structure will determine its evolution—and the more this internal structure will limit the evolutionary possibilities available to the overall organization.

A First Look at What's Inside the Organization

In biological evolution, fluctuations within the organism play a larger and larger role the more mature—and therefore complex—the organism is.[1] And in organizations, the more complex and mature the organization is, the more interactions *within* the organization will control its ability to respond to its environment.

In Chapter 2, we looked at how an organization adapts to a specific niche. When an organization becomes well adapted, it moves closer and closer to equilibrium and the entropy within the organization increases. Even though it may continue to serve its identified niche well, it nonetheless becomes less and less efficient at doing so. The more an organization dominates its niche and the more it moves toward equilibrium and suffers the effects of entropy, the more it focuses its attention on its internal structure and processes.

We need not look at the extremes to see how internal relationships drive the evolution of larger and more mature organizations. Take this rather simple comparison:

Sam and Sandra's Healthy Gnash chain has two stores, one downtown and one on the east side. Sam manages one store, Sandra the other. Each store has three employees. As Sandra's store is closing one night, Roberto, one of her employees, asks her if she's noticed that several customers have asked for a new type of low-fat cheese on their sandwiches. Sandra hasn't noticed, so when she gets home she asks Sam. "I dunno," Sam replies. "Let's both check it out." They decide not only to check with their employees but also to make sure they're handling the front counter themselves during the busiest times. They do so, and discover that the new cheese is indeed getting popular. The following Monday, the new cheese is featured, available for a small additional charge.

Five years have passed. Sam and Sandra had a good idea, so there are now twenty-seven Healthy Gnashes spread over twelve cities in the region. Most of them are franchises. Sam, now the CEO, gets a call from the manager of the Fresno store. It seems that customers have begun asking for a new multigrain bread that's being advertised in the area. Sam promises to look into it. He talks with Mel, his marketing chief. "It hasn't shown up in any of our focus groups," Mel says. "We'll be doing another round of them next month, so we'll add something on that." Then Sam asks Karen, who handles supplies for the chain, about the bread. "I'm sure we could get it, but it's new and hot and we won't get any price break on it. Tom [the comptroller] has been all over me to keep our costs under control, and this would really drive him up a wall. We might lose a little business, but unless you want a repeat of the flap we had over the fancy mustard last month we'd better just let this one go." So Sam waits until two months pass, at which time Mel says his data show that the new bread is popular in only a few of their locations. It's really not worth fooling with, Sam concludes.

A conventional analysis would concentrate on the internal bureaucracy in the second example. To an extent, it should. But if it stops there, it gives a misleading impression: Organizational life is not so simple as "getting rid of bureaucracy." An organization needs an internal structure.

As human beings, we tend to concentrate on the highly visible parts of animal evolution that have led to *Homo sapiens*. That means we look only at the last few seconds of the evolutionary football game. If we widen our view to include the rest of the game, we can gain a far more realistic picture of the development of internal structure.

Specifically, we can see the development of the eukaryotic cell. Somewhere around two billion years ago, this cell evolved from the bacteria and prokaryotic cells that preceded it. What made the eukaryotic cell special? All its predecessors had a simple structure in which the entire cell, or a series of identical cells, performed all the functions—much like a one-person business. But the eukaryotic cell was differentiated internally; it assigned different specialized functions to different parts of the cell. Then eukaryotic cells could combine with one another into new and far more complex organisms.[2] In short, it made possible all the complex world of visible living beings as we know it.

If the entirety of evolutionary progress has been made possible by the development of more and more complex internal structures, perhaps we should attempt to understand the issues this raises before determining that simplification is the solution to all organizational problems. Specifically, all structure, all evolution, all change result from the interaction of two forces: differentiation and integration. As authors Mihaly Csikszentmihalyi, Kevin Rathunde, and Samuel Whalen have put it:

> An integrated system is one in which the individual parts that make up the system are successfully interrelated and mutually reinforcing. A differentiated system, in contrast, is one in which the individual parts have unique or specialized functions. In a more process-oriented language, to integrate is to bring together parts, to organize or harmonize; to differentiate is to make distinctions among, to discriminate contrasts among, parts. . . .
> Common to all levels of analysis is the association

of integration with stability (constancy) and of differentiation with change. An optimal system is *complex,* that is, both integrated and differentiated. It is cohesive and stable yet able to adapt and change when necessary.[3]

This statement succinctly describes one of the most basic and enduring organizational questions: How does an organization integrate its various functions successfully while at the same time differentiating and maintaining the integrity of the individual functions? Or, what is the same thing in the long run, how does it balance the stability required to maintain itself with the dynamism necessary to evolve successfully?

So organizational success is not achieved just through simplification. An effective organization cannot help becoming complex. How does it achieve true complexity, that is, simultaneous differentiation and integration? And how does it accomplish this in an uncertain environment in which it must select and actualize certain potentials and not others? How does Healthy Gnash move successfully from a two-store operation to a regional one? Then, once it has defined its niche, how does it continue to adapt successfully to an uncertain and continually changing world?

When Healthy Gnash was new and small, it was integrated and relatively undifferentiated. Everyone reacted directly to customers. Everyone in each of the two operations also interacted directly with each other and shared functions. (Note the beginnings of differentiation, however: The only individuals from separate stores who interacted with each other were Sam and Sandra.) Roberto could point out an environmental change to Sandra; then she and Sam could immediately gather more data and make a decision.

In the larger and more mature Healthy Gnash, though, environmental input begins to encounter internal relationships. Mel has an established method for getting customer input. Karen has established suppliers. More than that, she has to deal with her relationship with Tom. And all of them retain vivid memories of the violent argument over adopting a fancy mustard from the month before.

Shorn of the detail, the essence looks like this. A small, "immature," largely undifferentiated organization is open to environmental input at every point, and this input gets heard because it competes with very little internal "noise." As the organization matures, however, it begins to limit the individuals and functions that transact with the environment—and once they receive information, that information must compete with a host of internal events and relationships for attention and action.

A Brief Reality Check

If you'd like to make the picture of Healthy Gnash more real in terms of your own organization, take a piece of paper and a pencil or pen and make some notes in answer to the questions below.

Suppose you come up with a really good idea. (If you can do so quickly, think of a very specific idea that would improve some aspect of your organization.) How do you go about getting your organization to use it? Is there a realistic process in place that will get your idea an honest hearing? If so, how does it work? How long does it take? If it gets adopted, what do you get for your efforts? If no useful process exists, how do you get your idea listened to? Who will listen to you? Who has enough clout to see that it is implemented? Formal program or not, does your idea get caught up in "the bureaucracy"? Is your boss a help or a hindrance to getting it implemented?

Now, the critical question: Does the organization have any mechanism, formal or informal, detailed or broad, for determining whether new ideas have potential and how to investigate those that do? It may be that the organization resists new ideas because it has no way of judging which ones have sufficient promise to be worth developing.

Keep these questions in mind as you travel through the rest of the book.

A Closer Look: Four Components of Organizations

How can you use evolutionary concepts like "maturity" and "complexity" to begin building an organization that can make helpful, efficient changes? About a year ago, a major business magazine published a cover feature on what large organizations can learn from small ones. It was remarkable in that it equated small, growing organizations, in which entrepreneurialism and opportunism must reign or else, with large, mature organizations that are attempting to deal realistically with large, complex markets. That makes great copy, but it avoids the basic issues. If successful evolution occurs when companies develop greater complexity (combining differentiation and integration), the long-run solution is hardly to regress to a more immature stage of evolution. Instead, organizations need to develop the ability to mature without suffering the ravages of internal hardening of the arteries (advancing entropy).

For those of us accustomed over the years to looking at organization charts, structure is constituted primarily by decisions on who does what and who reports to whom. After the impact first of TQM and now business process reengineering, structure may appear to be primarily an organization's processes, the steps that must be followed to produce the organization's outcomes.

Structure in organisms is created by the organism's need to assign functions to different parts *and* by its need to coordinate these parts with each other. The human body provides one way of doing this. While the brain makes constant decisions on what an individual human will do and say, the brain directly controls virtually none of the organs of actions and speech. It must receive information from organs specialized to receive environmental information, process it, then transmit directions to other organs specialized for speech or action.

Traditional organizational theory started with an understanding of organization much like this and built a specific model from it. In the model, an organization assigns functions to different units—marketing, manufacturing, sales, and so forth.

These functions must be clear and must not overlap among the units. A small number of these subunits, primarily marketing and corporate communications, are designed to secure information from or provide information to the environment. Most subunits, however, either carry out the organization's basic functions (product design, manufacturing, sales) or support or control these functions (quality control, finance).

To accomplish these goals, communication is sharply limited and occurs almost exclusively up and down the chain of command. Information on the state of the organization and the environment travels up. Direction about what actions to take travels down. No one should get or pass on any information that is not required to exercise some specific function. In this process, the executive determines what should be done and how well it is being done. Everyone else either helps him make the determination (staff) or carries out his decisions (line).

Despite the theory, no organization ever worked this way. And no organization in today's dynamic environment could conceivably work this way. So organizations are rightsizing, re-engineering, and reinventing themselves to structure themselves in other, different ways. But no amount of reinvention will alter the basic fact that organizations must develop an internal structure in order to exist and carry out their functions. And the more elaborate this internal structure becomes, the more an organization's evolution (or lack of it) will be determined by its structure rather than by events occurring in the environment.

We've seen that an organization can so dominate its niche that it becomes virtually a closed system. But this is an extreme case. What about less extreme cases, organizations that are succeeding and quite possibly growing? How do their internal structures affect their evolution?

The answer lies in a key concept of contemporary evolutionary theory that derives from systems theory. This concept is *autopoiesis*, "the characteristic of living systems to continuously renew themselves and to regulate this process in such a way that the integrity of their structure is maintained."[4]

Peter Senge put the same thought even more succinctly when he said, "the harder you push, the harder the system pushes back."[5] In fact, the defining characteristic of a system of any sort is this attempt to maintain the integrity of its structure—to push back when pushed upon, and to push back harder when pushed upon harder.

Any organism structures itself internally in a specific way and attempts to preserve this structure in the face of pressures to change. Human beings have perfectly acceptable sight during daylight, but at night its effectiveness drops off sharply. Since we must increasingly live and work (and fight) at night, there could be tremendous evolutionary pressure on our visual system to change. Over millions of years, humans might evolve two different visual systems, one for high light levels and one for very low levels. But we probably won't. We prefer to maintain the integrity of our existing visual structure, so we use lights of various kinds to make the night more like the day, or use infared devices that artificially expand our visual abilities.

Organizations use the same strategy. Chapter 2 pointed out the importance of equilibrium, the lowest energy state in which an organization can accomplish its basic goals. As the old saying that encapsulates this precise thought goes: "If it ain't broke, don't fix it."

Equilibrium primarily means not that an organization *uses* less energy but that it needs to import less energy in the form of resources. Chapter 1 pointed out the four visible costs of change—time, money, effort, and attention—and the fifth, less visible cost—the opportunity cost. The first four costs constitute the four basic resources available to any organization. Opportunity costs describe what might have been accomplished had the resources been spent more wisely. Together they describe a situation that all individuals and organizations are more familiar with than they would like to be: The more of any of these resources that an individual or organization consumes to achieve a given goal, the fewer of them that remain available to support other goals. Equilibrium describes, at least in theory and for stable systems, the internal structure that minimizes the opportunity costs of maintaining the integrity of the present structure.

General Motors provides three differing views on the ways in which an organization can seek or depart from equilibrium. Many writers (myself included) have hailed GM's development of the Saturn as one of the most significant evolutionary changes of the past two decades. So it is. Now that the Saturn is in full production, however, its tremendous costs to GM have become visible. Two of GM's bread-and-butter cars, the Chevy Cavalier and the Pontiac Sunbird, went basically unchanged for a decade because the money that might have been available for their redesign went into the Saturn (which, as I write, is at best barely profitable). And who knows how much the publicity given to the Saturn interfered with GM's attempts to get its other vehicles before the public eye?

During the same time period, GM employed a radically different strategy to get another small car into production. It formed NUMMI (New United Motors Manufacturing, Inc.) as a joint venture with Toyota, then basically turned over to Toyota a shuttered plant in Fremont, California. There, NUMMI has been building what is now the Geo Prizm—a virtual replica of the Toyota Corolla (which it also builds there). The Prizm has been a manufacturing success; *Consumer Reports* has consistently rated it substantially equal in quality to Corollas made in Japan. Commercially, it has been worth continuing but hardly profitable. Nonetheless, GM invested far fewer resources in NUMMI than it did in the Saturn and produced a car far sooner.

To truly understand equilibrium and maintaining the integrity of the existing structure, though, we have to look at what was happening at GM while Saturn and NUMMI were coming off the ground. The answer: virtually nothing. Saturn was intentionally isolated from mainstream GM; the parent organization continued as it had with substantially zero input from Saturn Motors. NUMMI was designed to help GM learn about Japanese manufacturing methods. GM managers were regularly rotated through Fremont. Then these managers and what they had learned were systematically ignored by GM. Through Smith's tenure as CEO and continuing into Stempel's, GM made the fewest and smallest changes possible in the way it operated, despite information it could have gained from its Saturn and (particularly) NUMMI experiences that its operations were notably inefficient. And many of the changes that did occur were made by individual plant managers who were isolated enough to get away with trying something new without affecting the basic structure of the corporation.

We've seen three specific reasons why successful change is both difficult and expensive: (1) The future is hard to predict; (2) change programs are often inadequate to the situation; and (3) only individuals can change. Now we can add a fourth reason: Organizations devote time, effort, money, and attention to preserving their current structures, and on the whole they do it successfully. All too often, this resistance to change gets described as the resistance of the current organizational culture and of recalcitrant individuals to change. Culture does matter; but culture never accounts for all of the resistance. *The underlying reason for the resistance is the total system's attempt to maintain its integrity.*

How does it do this? To simplify somewhat, an organization has six component systems: technology; processes, functions, and organizational structures; incentives; competence; culture; and information flow. These six component systems work together to maintain the overall organizational system as it is. Chapter 4 deals with information and its embodiment in culture. The remainder of this chapter provides a quick survey of the other four component systems and their part in the organization's attempt to maintain its current structural integrity.

The Technology Component

Two statements about technology are virtually incontrovertible:

1. *Organizations vary widely in their dependence on technology.* Insurance companies and government agencies with similar functions such as the Social Security Administration or the Internal Revenue Service depend absolutely on their computer systems to function. Oil and mining companies are equally dependent on both mechanical and electronic technology. On the other hand, commercial art firms and publishing houses can operate successfully without as extensive a technological base.

2. *No matter how dependent they have been in the past on their technology, virtually every organization is becoming more and more dependent on it as each day passes.* Technology in highly knowledge-work-intensive operations like those performed by advertising agencies and architectural firms is evolving to the point at

which without networked visualization and simulation systems the firms would simply be unable to compete.

Because of this, existing technology increasingly ties an organization to its current mode of operation. Major corporations (and government agencies) have been struggling for a decade with the problem of "legacy systems." These are the basic systems—payroll, accounts receivable, corporate information, claims processing, and so on and on—that not only function inefficiently by today's standards but lock the company into inflexible ways of operating. They do even more damage: They force workers and managers to spend increasing amounts of time attempting to work around them.

Technology cannot be separated from other aspects of organization. A company cannot simply pluck out its existing technology and slip in a replacement, as if it were changing razor blades or videotapes. Anyone who works in an organization that makes even minor changes in its computer systems discovers that these "minor" changes can have major impacts on how and how well work gets done. And if you follow the progress of client-server implementations through the computer press, you know about the downright trauma that companies often experience as they attempt to move to this new form of computer architecture. (We're not even counting the failed implementations. In one case, a state motor vehicle department took down its antiquated vehicle and driver registration system to install a new system—only to find that the new system didn't work at all.)

Is it any wonder that organizations keep trying to maintain their integrity by using existing technology instead of subjecting themselves to the risks of replacing it? Is it any wonder that new steel-making technology was utilized first by upstart minimills rather than by existing steel companies? Or that IBM and Digital, with their detailed knowledge of the technology required to make mainframes and minicomputers, are still attempting to catch up with upstarts like Compaq and Dell in the personal computer market?

The Processes, Functions, and Organizational Structures Component

Does it seem strange, perhaps an oversimplification beyond the permissible, to lump processes, functions, and organizational structures together? Certainly most of us are accustomed to thinking of them as very separate factors. But the three are a genuinely matched set; processes exist to accomplish functions, and the formal organizational structure reflects the organization's current way of relating processes and functions to each other and to the overall control system. In short, if an organization seriously attempts to change one, the change will without fail affect the other two. Want to create a new organizational architecture? You must begin by determining where functions will be placed, then identify the processes within and among these functions necessary to support them. Want to refine or re-engineer processes? You have to begin with function, and unless the process is trivially simple you will soon be examining how organizational structures affect it.

Lest this appear overly neat, let me provide a specific example all too real to companies that have attempted to implement TQM. Typically, implementation of TQM begins with the creation of teams to monitor and improve processes. And, typically, they produce successes—sometimes dramatic successes—for a year or eighteen months. Then, typically again, the whole effort begins to founder. Why? As teams go more deeply into processes, they find that these processes cross functional and organizational lines. When they attempt to deal with the processes, they run into a wall or, more exactly, a set of walls. These are the walls that separate different units and functions, the walls that they erect to preserve the integrity of their structure. At this point, the majority of organizations prefer to call it quits and either limit teams to strictly local processes or abandon teams altogether.

In the real world of organizations, function, process, and organizational structure are mutually reinforcing. Push on one and all three push back.

The Incentives Component

When an organization is established, it creates a set of formal and informal incentives. These strongly influence the initial culture of the organization. A technology organization that rewards technical excellence will attract and retain individuals who want to be rewarded for technical excellence. They, in turn, will shape the organization's formal and informal incentives. If the company adopts a TQM program, it will be shaped to fit existing incentives; while it may reward the use of TQM methods to identify customer needs, it will almost certainly reward the use of TQM to produce higher technical excellence and its implementation in manufacturing processes.

You may wonder why I mention TQM so frequently when it forms only one of many major change efforts over the past decade and a half. The answer is simple: TQM is both relatively recent and has been widely studied, which means that we know a great deal about its successes and failures. As I write this, rightsizing, reengineering, and self-managing teams are also popular, but we do not yet have enough data on them to permit the kinds of conclusions that can be drawn from TQM programs.

One federal agency implemented a far-reaching performance measurement system in the 1970s and early 1980s. Individual activities and functions were carefully rated and compared on a wide variety of quantitative measures. In the late 1980s, the agency decided to implement TQM. When it then formally disbanded TQM in the early 1990s, no measure of quality had been developed to supplant or complement the quantitative measures. Despite the ritual statements by executives and managers, workers and these same managers knew that their careers lived and died by the quantitative measures. Quality was never more than a nice-to-have add-on.

The great psychologist Abraham Maslow concluded years ago that workers and managers in a typical organization may not be as mentally healthy as one would like, but that they were very realistic about their work situations. Part of being realistic means understanding what the real incentives are and then using them to advance one's goals. Individuals either adapt to the incentives or leave. Those who remain and adapt then have every reason to maintain the incentives, which means that they have every reason to maintain the integrity of the existing structure of the organization that is tied to the incentives.

The Competence Component

Competence is the ability actually to do something, not to know about it, have great ideas about it, or understand what it means to do it (important as these are). Competence, in short, is the ability to execute successfully. Without the requisite competence, neither individuals nor organizations can function effectively.

Suppose an organization has functioned for years in a traditional, hierarchical mode. Then it decides to adopt self-managing teams. Assuming that every other aspect of the situation favors teams—an almost impossible assumption—the organization must still develop the competence required for successful team operation. "Bosses" must become "coaches" and "mentors." Individuals prized for a decade for their willingness to quietly follow orders must learn to manage themselves. In a situation where conflict had been strongly repressed, now everyone must develop the ability to bring conflict into the open and manage it. And individuals long accustomed to taking disputes to their supervisors must learn to negotiate these same disputes with their peers. The sheer shift in the competencies required is mind-boggling.

The impact of competence extends much further than this. Even for established companies, basic technologies keep changing. Polaroid has decided that it needs to move its core competence from chemistry to electronics; it would be difficult to imagine a more radical shift in competence. And what of phone and cable companies that have been handling copper wire forever but suddenly find themselves in the optical fiber business?

Yet again, we human beings largely enjoy doing what we know how to do and generally feel uncomfortable and incompetent when pushed to do something we don't know how to do. As a result, we tend to manage new efforts by taking a "that's nothing but . . ." approach to them. For instance, many industrial engineers and consultants have taken this approach to reengineering: It's nothing but what we've been doing all along. That may be true. It may also be one of the reasons that so many reengineering programs have returned results far short of expectations.

Finally, and as you would expect, every organization develops some competencies at the cost of not developing others. The currently popular phrase *core competence* captures some of this picture, but not all. Motorola was able to implement TQM as a viable competitive weapon faster than many of its competitors did because its workers and managers were already accustomed to a high level of worker participation in workplace decisions. But the company has had to spend millions to upgrade the educational competence of these same individuals, first to the seventh grade level and then to the eighth. GM was able to use its very high level of core technical excellence to produce the Northstar system as a clear competitive advantage of its high-end cars over their competitors. But its high-end cars still trail their Japanese counterparts significantly on most quality measures.

Just as too few organizations stop to identify their real incentives before attempting a change, they often forget to ask what their true competencies are. Then, when the change begins to falter, executives fall back on the old saws of resistance to change, union opposition, management shortsightedness, and poor motivation. They too seldom investigate whether managers and workers are able to do what the change demands that they do. The change fails or simply dies standing up, and the company returns to doing what it knows how to do.

A Brief Reality Check

Why not pause for a moment to make these ideas more concrete? Select one of the four components that push organizations to maintain the integrity of their current structure: technology; functions, processes, and organizational structure; incentives; or competence. Look at the results of your organization's attempts to change from the vantage point of one of these components. Specifically, if the organization has attempted a major change, did this component help or hinder the change? How? Did the organization consciously deal with the component?

What conclusions did you reach?

The Interrelationship of the Components

Each of these components is a separate system of its own, but each of them also reinforces each of the other components.

Technology cannot be separated from the functions, processes, and organizational structure organized around it, which cannot be separated from the incentives built into these systems, which in turn cannot be separated from the competence of the organization. (And none of these can be separated from either culture or information flow.)

On the other hand, the match between components is often less close than it might be. Because organizations tend to treat each of the components in isolation, they can easily make changes in one component that don't fit one or more of the other components. When an organization adopts either TQM process teams or self-managing teams, it appears to change only one component: functions, processes, and organizational structure. But the change will quickly affect competence (how will the teams get the increased competence that their members need?) and incentives (how will teams be rewarded for increased quality and productivity?). And if the organization begins to succeed with either form of team, it will quickly find that its existing technology does not fit the way that the teams operate.

All too often, the organization responds with mild shock that the change is having an impact far beyond one narrow area. Then it confronts the problem of what to do about this impact. If the change threatens seriously to upset the organization's equilibrium, the organization may simply abandon it, perhaps to pursue another promising and popular program (for instance, it may decide to drop self-managing teams and "do" reengineering instead). Or it may attempt to minimize the conflict by sharply restricting the change (for example, it may limit the areas in which the teams can function). Or it may make minimal changes in other components, such as adding team recognition to the existing individually oriented recognition program. Most rarely, it may see a sufficient payoff in the change to undertake modification of all the systems the change affects.

In the typical situation, the different component systems fit each other tolerably well and therefore support each other tolerably well. Taken together, these component systems (together with culture and information flow) both create the necessity for the organization to maintain its current form *and* are the means by which it does so.

Thus organizations, like complex biological organisms, attempt to maintain their current structures. The more complex either the organism or the organization is, the more its evolution—or lack of evolution—will be determined by the interactions of these internal structures rather than by the total organization's interaction with its external environment.

Four Components: The Lessons

No one can understand the full scope of an organization's ability to maintain its current structure without being familiar with the role of both culture and information flow described in Chapter 4. However, we can draw some clear lessons here about the nature and impact of its internal components.

1. Someone has said that any organization is perfectly constructed to produce exactly the results it does. Look carefully at your organization, particularly at the parts and characteristics that aren't working as well as you would like them to. Each of these plays a role in the total organization; each plays a part in the organization's successful ability to maintain itself. Instead of trying to change the parts that "don't work," you might better spend your time asking: Why, if they don't work, do they continue as they are? When you find the answer, you will understand your organization much more completely than you do now.

2. You may be under tremendous pressure to adopt new technology, or else. Perhaps you need to replace a legacy mainframe computing system with client-server technology. Perhaps it's networking and videoconferencing that's needed. Perhaps you're considering equipping your salespeople with portable computers containing CD-ROMs with extensive product information. None of these is simply a change in technology. Every one of them, at least if they're successful, will require changes in virtually every other component system in the organization. You will save yourself and your organization much time and grief if you ask up front: How will we need to change our functional alignment, our processes, and our organizational structure?

How will we need to change our incentives? What new competencies will we need to develop? You won't be able to anticipate all the answers to these questions, but you'll avoid the shock of having to face them for the first time *after* you've begun to change the technology.

3. Functions, processes, and organizational structures have received so much attention in recent years that it appears superfluous to talk about them here. But incentives? That's a different matter. The most consistently unasked question in all organizational change is: Why would they want to do this instead of what they're doing now? Again, if you ask it when you begin to plan a change, you will find that it rapidly deepens your appreciation of the real-world situation. Dealing with that question may cause you to modify the change or perhaps even to abandon it. Better to do it at the beginning, not after you jump into the sea and find that the waters simply refuse to part.

4. The most important lesson is this: Since the internal structure of a complex organization has a dramatic impact on its evolution, then the change that will work best is the change that best draws on the strengths of the existing systems. The fundamental objection I make to many individuals who tout transformational and cultural change is that they systematically ignore this basic truth. I'm sure there are times when an organization has gotten so out of touch with its competitive environment that it has no choice but to completely reinvent itself. I'm equally sure that this is *not* a desirable situation. An organization needs to utilize every possible existing strength when it proposes to change.

4

Playing the Information Game

We tend to think of biological evolution as the progress from one kind of plant or animal to another. In other words, evolution seems to be about bodies. In reality, bodies are simply the visible results of evolution. Biological survival and evolution are all about *information*. And organizational survival and evolution are also about *information* and knowledge and their embodiment in the organization's culture.

Evolution, Information, and Culture

DNA, the source of both stability and evolution, is information. Science writers refer to the genetic "code"—and what is a code but a form of information? DNA passes genetic information from one generation to another. When the genetic information passes on unchanged, the species remains the same. When the genetic information is altered—the real meaning of "mutation"—it creates the possibility that a new species may arise.

A human being comes into existence when a single sperm and a single egg, both microscopic, unite. The amount of matter in either is insignificant. Yet the amount of information contained in each defies comprehension. From the information carried in the egg and sperm, a complete human being gets built. Out of literally millions of possibilities, a unique person emerges. Somehow, millions of decisions are made and implemented in the process from fertilized egg through embryo to birth.

This ought to suggest the awesome power of information. But the story of information in evolution only begins here. When an organism comes into existence, it enters a world where its use of information will determine its destiny. An organism finds food or starves, reproduces or not, as a result of its ability to acquire and use information from its environment. An amoeba may move toward "food" without ever knowing that it has received and acted on information, but it gets and uses the information nonetheless.

Very primitive organisms gain very little "knowledge" throughout their lifespans, even though the lifetime of organisms such as the amoeba is theoretically infinite. As organisms grow more complex, however, this begins to change. Individual animals not only learn how to cope with the environment but pass this learning on from generation to generation. Predators teach their young how to hunt; raccoons teach their young to wash food; otters teach their young to play. This constitutes a major step. Instead of being processed automatically by what we call instincts, information is now processed by knowledge—a very different process.

When evolution arrives at human beings, however, the use of knowledge takes a quantum jump. While higher animals may in some sense develop a "culture," only humans have developed culture as an extension of evolution itself. The amount of knowledge and information encoded in even the most "primitive" human culture staggers the imagination.

Consider this brief and very revealing example of the complexity of knowledge and information in human culture. Researchers in artificial intelligence (AI) hoped to develop expert systems that would contain common sense. A funny thing happened along the way, however. They reached the astounding conclusion that if what we call common sense were reduced to rules, we would each have millions and perhaps billions of rules telling us how to go about the ordinary business of life.

What does this have to do with evolution and culture? What we call common sense is the basic information on how to live life successfully that every culture passes on from generation to generation. And it forms the base for the much more extensive knowledge and information embodied in urbanized cultures and in each of us that keeps us from having to learn basic knowledge over and over again in each new generation. (You may not have enjoyed learning the multiplication table, but compare that with the effort that would be required to *create* the multiplication table!)

Just as DNA embodies the information needed to create a human being from an egg and a sperm, so culture embodies the knowledge required to create an American or an aborigine from an infant human being. And that leads us directly to organizations, because what we call an organization is more than anything else a pattern of knowledge and an information flow made visible.

Knowledge and Information: a Matched Pair

You've read, endlessly I suspect, about the importance of "knowledge" work and the importance of information in organizations. Unfortunately, very few writers clarify the distinction between knowledge and information. In a nutshell, this is it:

> *Knowledge consists of the mental models we have that enable us to select and use information to accomplish our purposes.*

Individuals and organizations have knowledge when they can determine (1) what action could be taken, (2) when it could be taken, and (3) what information is relevant to decisions concerning the action. This knowledge is encoded in mental models of the world and how it works, and these enable the individuals and organizations to understand and carry out their purposes in their environments. The raw material of knowledge is ideas, but ideas by themselves don't constitute knowledge. An idea becomes knowledge only when an individual or organization can use it to carry out some purpose.

Information is no more or less than the data or facts that individuals and organizations are able to use to carry out these purposes.

What does this mean?

One of the clearest examples of knowledge as a mental model is the distinction made over thirty years ago by Douglas MacGregor between Theory X and Theory Y managers. Each of these theories is a different mental model of human behavior at work that enables a manager to carry out his or her purposes. And the information a manager will use to make decisions differs significantly between the two models.

Here is another broader example. Using its knowledge, an organization may consider entering a new market. It may then gather the information that will help it decide which market to enter. No amount of information on potential markets is of any use to it, however, unless it has the knowledge to assess the information and use it to accomplish its purposes. An organization with a strong technical culture may look for information about the technical sophistication of potential competitors' products. Another organization considering entering the same markets may look first for information on distribution channels. In each case, the organization works from a mental model that tells it what information is important to it.

In a very real sense, the visible organization—including its technology, its functions, processes, and organizational structure, its incentives, its competence, and certainly its culture—is its knowledge made visible. How successfully an organization competes, however, depends in large part on how it uses this knowledge and how it gets the information it needs. For the rest of the book, we will talk not about information in the abstract but about an organization's *information flow*. This information flow contains both the facts and the ideas that the organization knows how to use, or is willing to consider, to accomplish its purposes. It does not contain either facts or ideas that appear irrelevant to these purposes. The standard it uses to distinguish between relevant facts and ideas and irrelevant ones will, to a significant extent, determine its competitive success.

Culture: Knowledge and Information About Behavior, Values, and Perspectives

On one level, the culture of an organization is its visible behaviors—the preferred ways of acting of the organization's members. When a serviceman from the old IBM showed up, he was wearing a coat and tie. So was anyone representing EDS. These customs exemplified the specific ways in which members of these organizations were expected to behave. During the same time, managers at Dr. Pepper headquarters who didn't show up for barbecues, and who weren't wearing jeans, were out of sync with one of this organization's basic customs.

A Brief Reality Check

To help make this idea of culture as organizational custom real for you, take a moment to describe some of the key behaviors in your organization. It might help to ask these questions:

When an outsider first meets someone from your company, what will his or her first impressions be? Will the individual from your company be impeccably dressed, dressed in normal business attire, or casually dressed? Will the individual be extremely friendly, courteous, or slightly reserved? What behaviors will strike an outsider first?

Now, what do you expect when you meet with someone from within your company? How is the individual dressed? How friendly is he or she? More important, what do you expect the individual to talk about; what are the important topics? And can you depend on him or her to help you get what you need?

When you've answered these questions, reflect for a minute on the image that this behavior projects. And then reflect on how deep the behaviors go. Do they really reveal what's important, or are they just a decorative veneer on the real culture of the organization?

Genuine customs reflect the underlying *values* of the organization. On one level, values express what the organization considers important enough to merit constant attention. An organization that values technical excellence may also be concerned about customer satisfaction, but, in any conflict between the two, members are expected to choose technical excellence. An employee at Nordstrom or Fedex pays attention first to whatever is necessary to satisfy the customer—and then to everything else.

At an even deeper level, however, an organization's culture expresses strong, often unstated assumptions about the answers to such questions as: Who are we? What should we do? What is the world really like? The answers to these and similar questions constitute the basic *perspective* that characterizes the organization—and this perspective, more than anything else, creates the organization's culture. This perspective is the "deepest" information in the organization.[1]

In the "good old days," IBM's perspective on itself and its world was simple: Sell top management and then provide the organization with world-class service. The people who counted from the perspective of an IBM salesman weren't the computer people; let competitors deal with them. IBM's target was the CEO. And once the CEO bought IBM, it became the job of IBM to demonstrate that he had made a wise decision by keeping his company's computers (including their software) up and running. When the world changed, IBM had tremendous difficulty adapting to the world of personal computers; from their perspective, they couldn't understand computing that the CEO didn't control and that valued quality and price far more than service.

L. L. Bean, the catalogue sales company, has an equally clear perspective on what the company is about. In one of his first fliers, mailed in 1912, L. L. Bean said: "I do not consider the sale a success until the goods are worn out and the customer still satisfied." That perspective has remained a powerful one. While other catalogue merchandisers may breathe down its neck, L. L. Bean remains the company to beat.

An organization's basic perspective doesn't arrive out of thin air or in the CEO's briefcase. It is created by the organization's experience of what has worked for it. IBM's perspective on its business—sell the CEO and provide highly visible, effective service—worked not just for years but for decades. L. L. Bean's perspective—satisfy the customer at all costs—has worked for almost a century.

A Brief Reality Check

In the last exercise, you looked at the visible behaviors or customs that characterize your organization. Now you want to look beneath these customs to the values that support them.

These three questions may help:

1. What is your job? What do you have to do to be really successful? Do you succeed by pleasing customers, pleasing your boss, not making waves, or . . . ?
2. What makes your organization different from all others? What is its distinctive perspective on itself?
3. If things began to change, what characteristics of your organization would you fight hardest to retain? Which ones would you most quickly give up?

These questions touch only the surface of your organization's culture, of course, but they provide valuable clues to some of its core values and perspectives.

Does something begin to sound familiar about an organization's perspective? It should, because perspective is the intellectual/values/culture side of organizational integrity. The harder you push a system the harder it pushes back. If the system is an organizational system, it not only pushes back but it tells you that you're wrong! And from its perspective, you are.

In short, an organization's "culture" embodies the core behaviors, the core values, and the core assumptions that maintain its integrity as a system.

This has immense implications for "cultural change" or "transformational change": When we say that we are going to change or transform an organization's culture, we are saying that we are going to attack its integrity as a system. No more. No less.

Yet Another Brief Reality Check

If you did the last reality check, look at your answer to the third question: If things began to change, what characteristic of your organization would you fight hardest to retain? Relax for a moment and close your eyes. Visualize someone calling you to a meeting and announcing that this characteristic interferes with the organization's plans for itself and is going to be changed immediately.

How do you react? What do you feel? What, if anything, do you want to do?

You have just experienced how a system that is being pushed feels and why it pushes back. If you are a "change agent," you have just experienced what all those individuals who "resist change" probably felt when you announced your newest program. In short, you have just experienced how a human or organizational system feels when it believes its integrity is threatened.

Another (Very) Brief Reality Check

Just ask yourself: Does your reaction to someone wanting to change an important characteristic of your organization affect how you feel about those individuals who are resisting your latest change? If you're on the other side, does it help you understand why you are or are not resisting the latest change?

These considerations add another dimension to the conclusions of Chapter 3: If you want change to succeed, build on what is already there and make the fewest possible changes to an organization's technology, functions, its processes, and organizational structures, its competence, its incentives, *and* its culture. In other words, the organization's culture *matters* to people.

Finally we come to the heart of the organization: the information flow that maintains its technology; its structures, processes, and functions; its incentives; its competence; and its culture.

What "Information" Really Means

We often speak of "information" as if it were an objective quantity, something that can be measured like lima beans or counted like elephants. This misleading view gets strengthened every time we speak of human feedback as analogous to the operation of a thermostat, or describe the human communication process as a problem in coding and decoding a message that is similar to encoding and decoding a radio signal. If this were the case, communicating information would be nothing more than a technical problem: If we could just "be objective about this" and "listen to each other," we could all communicate successfully.

The problem goes much deeper than these analogies suggest. When individuals speak of information in an organization they tend (1) to speak largely of data rather than of information, and (2) to describe information as though it were a single entity easily understood by everyone. Both these approaches are misleading, and both are misleading for essentially the same reason.

Remember, data equal facts. The temperature didn't rise above freezing today in Fargo, North Dakota. GM's profits for the third quarter this year are 12 percent higher than they were for the same period last year. These constitute statements about some specific state of affairs—that's what makes them facts. On any given day, each one of us gains access to dozens or, more likely, hundreds of facts like these. But no fact automatically becomes information and thus part of an individual's or an organization's information flow. Neither does an idea automatically become part of the flow. Remember, the information flow of an organization contains the facts and the ideas that the organization knows how to use to accomplish its purposes. It does not contain either facts or ideas that appear irrelevant to these purposes.

Precisely what does this mean? It means that individuals and organizations completely determine the facts and ideas that will make up their information flow, and they determine this by how they use these facts and ideas. Whether some fact is information has nothing to do with whether it's contained in a formal, automated management information system (MIS), or in monthly reports to the Corporate Office, or released by the Corporate Communications Office, or used in a training course, or in an Executive Leadership Workshop, or. . . . Whether an idea will be treated as knowledge has nothing to do with who expressed it or how interesting it is. Why? Because individuals and organizations define the information flow by the purpose for which they use it, not by the form in which it appears.

Every major newspaper carries the listing for the New York Stock Exchange. Does that listing constitute information? The majority of the people who buy the paper skip those pages. They see the listing as so much irrelevant data. A few turn to the listing. Do they read all of it? Of course not. Instead, they focus on one or a few stocks to see how those stocks are doing. Even then, the purpose for which they read the listing varies from individual to individual. Only an individual, or an organization composed of individuals, can turn data and ideas into information and knowledge.

The fundamental purposes of individuals and organizations change very slowly. An individual may start off in her early twenties to "make a living." A business may be formed to refurbish antique and superluxury automobiles. Twenty years later, the person making a living may have held fifteen different positions with four different companies, but she is still engaged in making a living. The business that began refurbishing automobiles has moved three times into larger and better quarters and has begun doing modifications to these automobiles, but it's still following its original purpose.

An information flow is defined by an organization's purposes, and over time it affects these purposes. In the short run, however, this flow affects not the purposes themselves but how they are carried out. Because of this, most information that moves through an organization falls into one of five broad classes: It (1) transmits values; (2) provides direction in the form of goals, objectives, and expectations; (3) provides feedback on results; (4) transmits competence; and (5) triggers action.

Information About Behavior, Values, and Perspectives

The daily operation of the organization's culture provides the fundamental information on basic values (and, though usually implicitly, on the perspectives that underlie the values). I still remember an event that happened well over a decade ago, when I had just moved to a senior management position in a new field organization. My second day there, another senior manager asked me to drop by his office. Our conversation was short and simple. He said, "We're always honest with one another around here. I know you'll be the same way." That brief statement transmitted very clear information about a key organizational value.

Organizational value and vision statements enjoyed great popularity at the end of the 1980s and into the early 1990s. Unfortunately, their success never equaled their popularity, primarily because both vision and values are created by and transmitted through the day-to-day actions of the individuals in the organization. They can be changed, but producing a list of values to hang on corporate walls doesn't begin to generate enough impetus to change them. Valuing innovation or envisioning an innovative, flexible company means little if experience has taught workers and managers that they get ahead by never, ever making waves. That's a value based on experience— and values based on experience usually win.

Even when most of an organization's members believe it should change, its cultural values are often so deeply imprinted that these same members can't believe it really will change. The CEO may honestly intend for the corporation to value innovation, but unless he can *demonstrate* again and again that innovation really will be supported, the ingrained value of "don't make waves" will overcome his best efforts.

Whether it works for stability or change, information about the organization's behaviors, values, and perspectives continually circulates among its members. New employees and managers get indoctrinated, formally and informally. Long-term members reinforce the values to one another, inform newer members about how things *really* are, and recount cynically what happened eight years ago when the organization tried to make the same change.

Information About Goals, Objectives, and Expectations

Whatever else they do, organizations must keep all the individuals and units that comprise them moving in the same direction. They cannot permit marketing to design a five-year warranty, sales to promise speedy delivery no matter what, or manufacturing to cut corners to meet delivery dates. Fundamental information about direction gets transmitted in myriad ways, from formal directives to casual conversation in break rooms and rest rooms. A department head calls in one of his managers and makes it clear that the upgraded graphics package will be ready for release in sixty days, no matter what. An executive casually mentions to a division chief that her people appear to be spending too much time on upgrading existing lines and not enough on true development.

Organizational goals always imply the more specific objectives required to attain them and expectations about what constitutes successful achievement of the goals and objectives. Some expectations are transmitted through formal standards and objectives: for example, 80 percent of customer problems to be solved on the first telephone call, full payback on any new technology within eighteen months. Far more often, expectations are more general and unstated. When the sales manager "encourages" her sales force to "sell harder" to existing accounts, she may never mention any specific increase in sales as a target. If a salesperson "sells harder," must he increase sales 10 percent, 30 percent, or simply create greater receptivity among his customers for the company's services? People may never know until someone fails to meet expectations; only then may the expectations become more concrete.

Information on goals, objectives, and expectations flows constantly through an organization, both formally and informally. The more open the channels of communication are, the greater the chance that formal and informal information will match. The reverse is also true: When communication is restricted, formal and informal channels often begin to carry very different information. "Hello, Bob? Yeah—I just wanted to tell you not to pay too much attention to the talk from Corporate on the big reengineering program. The word this quarter is increase revenues by at least 10 percent, no matter what. Got that? Good."

Information as Feedback

Feedback constitutes perhaps the most critical day-to-day form of information in organizations. Unfortunately, *feedback* is also the most overused and least understood term in the management vocabulary. Managers say to workers (or to other managers who report to them), "I want to give you some feedback," particularly at annual performance reviews, and proceed to judge their performance. The department gets a thick printout at the end of the month summarizing productivity, quality, and timeliness. At the end of the year, the division gets a complete profit and loss statement for the year. And we unthinkingly call all this feedback.

Time out. Feedback can take many forms, but the form that must exist for organizations to function effectively or else is this:

Feedback must contain specific information on (facts about) performance that the performer receives in time so as to be able to change that performance.

We owe much to the quality movement for its great contribution to our understanding of feedback. It stressed (1) that feedback should be generated by processes themselves, rather than by an external source, and (2) that feedback should come directly to the performers.

When individuals, units, and organizations get specific, objective, and timely information about the results of their performance, they have the power to change that performance. Conversely, when information on performance is generalized (for instance, buried in overall summaries), filtered through staff departments or levels of management, or delayed—well, individuals, units, and organizations just keep on doing what they've been doing. And this tendency is reinforced by a well-worn dictum in most organizations: If no one is griping at you, you're doing OK.

This concern with feedback has an even deeper level, one that—at least in the opinion of Mihaly Csikszentmihalyi—is deeply rooted in human evolution. Dr. Csikszentmihalyi, professor of psychology at the University of Chicago, has spent his career investigating what he calls "flow" experiences. When an individual is in this flow state, he or she produces at the highest level possible. Circumstances that promote the flow state have many characteristics; one of these characteristics is that the individual gets immediate, usable feedback on his or her progress toward goals. Conversely, when the environment fails to provide this feedback, the individual loses the ability to perform consistently at a high level.[2]

In short, nothing determines how well individuals and units succeed at achieving their goals and objectives more potently than the presence or absence of effective feedback.

Information That Increases Competence

As organizations rely more and more on "knowledge work" for competitive advantage, information designed to increase competence becomes a greater part of the total information flow. An assembly-line worker in a traditional plant requires relatively little information to perform his job competently. A short training course and some tips from more experienced workers will meet his training needs nicely—at least in theory. As more and more plants adopt quality methods, however, the amount of information required to operate competently rises sharply. Many automotive plants, particularly those run or influenced heavily by Japanese companies, now spend more on worker training each year than traditional plants used to spend over a worker's lifetime. And daily or weekly meetings are designed to pass on the learning acquired by one individual or team to others.

As the nation's output has increasingly become devoted to high-tech, high-touch operations, the sheer volume of information required to develop and maintain competence has been rising dramatically. Perhaps the epitome of this trend is the research scientist working in genetic engineering who has to run just to keep up with the advances in the field—and then run even faster in the race to get products to market in a hotly competitive market. Most of the information she receives is directly related to building and maintaining her competence. Or think of the attorney involved in intellectual property law in telecommunications, which may be changing even faster than genetic science.

Whether the company manufactures automobiles, litigates intellectual property rights, or advises clients on local-area networking, it must increasingly find ways to keep flowing the kind of information that will develop and maintain competence.

Information That Triggers Action

All other forms of information are useless unless they ultimately support taking some action or deciding not to take it. Individuals and organizations have purposes so that they can make changes in the real world. To accomplish this, values, direction, feedback, and competence aren't enough. There must also be information that triggers action, that gives the individual or organization the information it needs to take a specific action.

What kinds of information trigger action?

- The information a speaker gets about his audience so he can make an effective presentation
- The information a company obtains about a new technology so as to decide whether or not to use it
- The information a manager gets about the mood of her boss today so as to weigh the practicality of discussing problem areas with him

- The information an engineer gets to determine which of several competing workstations will best meet the needs of his department

This information needs to flow constantly throughout the organization. The programmers fighting desperately to have software ready for the new computer system need to know immediately if the system will be delayed for a month. At least as important, information must flow *into* the organization. If an airline is planning to expand its service to several cities, it needs to know the probability that the economy is heading toward recession.

Change and the Flow of Information

Whether as values, direction, feedback, competence, or a trigger to action, information is made up of ideas and data that support a current individual or organizational purpose. Whether a given idea or fact becomes part of the information flow depends almost entirely on its relationship to the existing state of the organization. Alternatively put, the existing state of the organizational system defines what will be information for it. And that has immense implications for both stability and change in organizations.

Paul Ingrassia and Joseph B. White's superb book *Comeback* provides one of the clearest and most dramatic examples possible of the rejection of data that couldn't be converted into information. In 1977, a GM engineer named Ricard began to study Toyota's production methods carefully. The next year, he addressed 150 GM executives and told them what he had found: Toyota workers could change a massive stamping die in three and a half minutes. At that time, GM workers took eight hours to perform the same task.

If the simplistic, "objective" understanding of information were true, what would the executives have done? They would have welcomed the information and bombarded Ricard with questions on how Toyota managed to accomplish this—so their workers could learn to do likewise. Is that what happened? Not at all. One executive suggested that Ricard was mistaken; Ricard assured him that he was not. The executive's response was pithy and to the point: "You're lying."

At that point, in Ingrassia and White's words, Ricard's peers "dismissed him with tirades about the cheap yen and coolie labor."[3] So much for thinking that Ricard's data automatically constituted information.

For the past decade, picking on GM has been a basic sport of management writers. No wonder; GM has gone around most of the time with a prominent KICK ME sign on its organizational backside. The fact is, though, that GM simply provides a large and very visible example of what happens in every organization. The more an organization becomes successfully established in its niche, the more it selects specific technologies, functions, processes, and organizational structures, and the more it develops specific incentives and competencies, the more it will filter the ideas and data available to it from both inside and outside. And it will filter these ideas and data on the basis of its current purposes. Almost never does an organization fail to change because it lacks either ideas or data. It fails because it cannot or will not fit them to its current purposes.

Information Flow and Purpose

The information flow of an organization contains the facts and ideas that the organization knows how to use to accomplish its purposes. It does not contain facts or ideas that appear irrelevant to these purposes. Up to this point, we have largely ignored the purposes of individuals. The time has arrived to remedy this oversight. The remedy is simply stated:

> *Organizations do not have purposes. Only individuals can have purposes.*

Just as the fiction that organizations can change blinds us to the reality that only individuals can change, so speaking of organizational purposes can obscure the fact that only individuals have purposes. These purposes may be more or less closely related to the "purposes" of the organization or the "purposes" of the organizational unit, but they are ultimately the purposes of the individual who holds them. When the individual in the story above called Ricard a liar, he was speaking *as* a GM executive, but he was speaking *from* his individual purposes.

Have you ever worked in a large organization that rotated managers through positions every two or three years? If so, you know how evanescent "organizational" purposes can be. A speaker at a Department of Defense conference on quality in the mid-1990s commented that no officer ever got promoted because he dutifully completed the work of his predecessor. The same logic applies to any organization in which managers rotate. And in any organizational situation, "This department is committed to . . ." or "This division will concentrate on . . ." are both so much window dressing for "I intend to . . ." and/or "My boss expects me to. . . ."

When a strong manager remains in a job for years, like Robert Galvin at Motorola or Jack Welch at GE, he may impose his purposes on the organization with relative success. But he can do this only to the extent that his purposes serve the purposes of each individual in the organization. At any moment, an organization's "purpose" is a mix—part polyphony, part cacophony, but seldom harmony—of the individual purposes of all its members.

If facts and ideas enter the information flow only when they become relevant to someone's purposes, and if ultimately only individuals have purposes, then the information flow in an organization is ultimately determined by the purposes of the individuals within it. In particular, this applies to any ideas or facts that might change the current state of the organization.

Organizations can establish information systems that force certain facts to be captured. These systems may be automated, as are the dozens of accounting and financial reports that flow through the typical organization. They may be partially or even totally manual, as are the quarterly reports on activities that many managers give regularly to their executives. But, of a certainty, these established systems capture only established, preselected information. They may provide a warning—that market share or revenue per product has dropped, for instance—but if the change is caused by changing external conditions, they will not provide information on what is happening or why. And, with all these limitations on the internal flow of facts, very few organizations have any systematic internal flow of ideas.

Substantially all information on new conditions is provided by human beings, and each human being has a purpose in providing, or withholding, this information. This means that all information, no matter how broad or extensive it may have been in its origin as fact, is highly local, because it becomes information only when a specific individual selects it to achieve his or her purposes.

This brings us back to evolution and its use of information. During the history of the planet, dramatic changes have occurred. Meteors hit, volcanoes covered the land around them with lava, ice ages came and went. We speak of the impact of these events on species and evolution, but that commits the same fallacy as speaking of organizations as changing. Species may remain the same, but change (mutation) always happens first at the individual level. Whether the change is adaptive will depend solely—*solely*—on its usefulness in the immediate environment of the individual. That little flowerfly in Chapter 2 that feeds on aphids couldn't care less about global conditions. Nor will he ever respond to them—except as they may affect the availability of aphids in his immediate neighborhood.

Human beings differ from other animals in several critical ways, but not in this one. What enters the information flow and what remains an unacknowledged fact or idea depends ultimately on its impact on the local purposes of an individual. These purposes may be more or less related to the purposes of the organization at large. They may be shared by a large number of individuals. But they will always be individual purposes, and individuals will identify and determine whether to pass on information in accordance with them.

This whole picture then becomes ever more complex because organizations of any size structure themselves into internal units, giving us not only the purposes of individuals and entire organizations but the purposes of teams, work groups, departments, and divisions. To the impact of these we now turn.

5

It's What's Inside That Counts

The more an organism divides itself into separate internal functions, the more the interaction between these functions will determine its evolution (or nonevolution). The more an organization divides itself into separate internal functions, the more the interaction between these functions—and between the individuals in them—will determine its evolution (or nonevolution).

The previous two chapters looked at the internal structure of organizations in terms of its six components. Now we look at the internal structure in terms of its organization into subordinate units based on their functions. The goal? To see how this form of internal structure influences the organization's ability to evolve successfully.

How Internal Structure Affects Organizational Change

All organizations of any size have highly developed internal organizational units based on functions—finance, marketing, manufacturing, and all the rest. These units share the six component subsystems of the larger organization: technology; functions, processes, and organizations; incentives; competence;

culture; and information flow. They also possess their own more or less unique versions of each of these components:

- Different units within an organization may have very different *technologies*. Consider this example: Except for the budget people who use highly sophisticated spreadsheets, the finance department uses computers to support clerical and semiclerical processes that have not changed significantly for years. On the other hand, product design's computers, which cannot talk with finance's computers, support very complex and generally high-level design processes. Although sales personnel use a large product database to match products with customer needs, the center of life for each salesperson is his or her personal contact database. Not only does this personal database not link up with either finance or engineering, it is never shared even with the sales department. And these differences are all *within* one basic type of technology—computers.

- Different units within the organization have very different *functions* (that goes without saying), *processes*, and *organizational structures*. Finance has very detailed processes supported by a highly developed control structure. Product design has few formal processes, most of which are out of date and simply ignored, a very loose supervisory structure, and virtually no internal organizational structure. Sales has some set procedures for making new contacts and servicing lapsed accounts, but most salespeople ignore these, and no one complains so long as they make their quotas.

- Different units within the organization have very different *incentives*. In finance, the dominant incentive is simple: Clerks are recognized and rewarded, first, for not making mistakes and, second, for the number of documents processed per hour. In product design, what pays off is disciplined creativity as reflected in workable designs. In sales, the bottom line is dollar sales per month.

- Different units within the organization have different *competencies*. Again, this almost goes without saying. Financial managers must be good at details and at control. Product design managers must understand how to further practical creativity and then get out of the way. Sales managers must be effective at "motivation."

• Because of all this, different units within the organization have very different *cultures*. You can quickly tell finance people from product design people at an office party, and no one would ever mistake an individual from either of these departments for someone from sales.

• Finally, different units within the organization have very different kinds of knowledge and use *information* in very different ways. Finance wants precise, auditable feedback about financial results. Product design people are far more interested in the newest trends and techniques, and want to ensure that their competencies are keeping up with these trends. Individual salespeople want to know cumulative dollar sales, for themselves and for every other salesperson.

In short, each internal unit of an organization attempts to maintain its integrity against pressures originating not only from outside the organization but also from other units within the organization. This has an additional dimension. Internal units do not just attempt to maintain themselves; they attempt to maintain themselves in constant interaction with other internal units. What happens in an organization is at least as much a product of the struggles between the various parts of the organization as it is a struggle with various environmental pressures. These struggles directly affect the ability of the organization to change in a variety of ways. They may create change that furthers the goals of one or a few units but that handicaps the organization as a whole. They may impede the attempts of the organization as a whole to change. The struggles may also divert the organization's attention and so use up its energy that it becomes paralyzed and unable to deal with the extensive changes that are occurring in its environment. In short, organizations tend to spend large amounts of attention on the interactions occurring within them.

Back to the example of the finance, design, and sales departments—except that we now substitute manufacturing for sales. The chief of manufacturing sends one of his cost accountants to a seminar on activity-based costing (ABC). ABC differs from traditional cost accounting in one highly significant way: Costs are allocated to the units that cause the costs ("drivers") rather than to the units that actually spend the money.

The accountant returns from the seminar and excitedly reports to the chief of manufacturing. The organization theoretically has a policy that once a product has been released to manufacturing the design is frozen. In practice, product design keeps making changes that the front office approves, and these changes drive up the manufacturing costs of the products. In the current system, the costs are allocated to manufacturing, which must constantly explain these "cost overruns." If the organization were to install ABC, the accountant explains, the costs would be allocated where they belong—to product design.

The chief of manufacturing gets the point and begins to campaign for ABC. The chief of product design finds out about the campaign and begins his own. He knows that ABC will result in a significant rise in his department's costs, and he has no intention of letting this happen. After all, if it weren't for the constant pressure on his people to cut design time, they wouldn't have to make so many changes after the designs were released to manufacturing.

What about the chief of finance? Basically, he doesn't care. The current system captures the costs; it doesn't matter to him where they're allocated. Besides, he's involved in an update of the payroll system that's not going as well as the CEO wants. He lets it be known that he doesn't really want to change the cost accounting system, but if somebody wants to pony up a half-dozen personnel slots for him to implement the new system. . . .

Does the scenario have something to do with satisfying customers, reducing operating costs, or increasing stockholder value? Hardly. Does it help the organization focus on changes in its markets and the environment in general so that it can anticipate or at least respond to these changes? Not at all. The infighting over whether to change the cost accounting system diverts attention away from the world outside the organization and focuses it instead on the organization itself. The result? Either the organization fails to change, or it changes in ways that have little to do with its ability to respond to its environment.

When the Organization Becomes the Environment

What's going on here? We've seen that complexity is *differentiation* of function *integrated* into an overall unity. Evolution depends both on increasing differentiation and on the ability to integrate that differentiation. Human beings are extremely complex beings, each of us operating as a single entity, even though our bodies are differentiated into lungs, feet, elbows, and all the rest. We know from experience how important integration is. Cancer constitutes an extreme form of the breakdown of integration; a cancerous growth has no use for the rest of the body. Far less extreme failures of integration plague us every day: upset stomachs that won't process food for the rest of the body; headaches that interfere with effective vision and thought; muscle strains that can make even simple movements painful.

The internal structure of organizations creates just these same opportunities for differentiation to take precedence over integration. The struggle over whether to adopt ABC cost-accounting methods may be something like the competition for oxygen between the brain and the stomach after a full meal. The critical point, though, is this: When an organization differentiates itself into an extensive internal structure, it becomes the environment within which its internal units compete for resources.

Although textbooks seldom put it this way, one function of a traditional, hierarchical organization has always been to control this competition, to impose integration by fiat. In very stable organizations operating in stable environments, this generally works. In dynamic organizations in dynamic environments, however, this imposed integration works far less effectively. Just as much traditional organizational theory was directed at controlling internal competition, much organizational rethinking over the past two decades has been attempting to find alternative ways to accomplish this. Vision, mission, and values, for instance, have been proposed primarily as a way of integrating differentiated and relatively autonomous subunits of the organization.

This internal differentiation and competition causes a variety of problems. First, it diverts the attention of the organization as a whole from its competitive environment. This particularly characterizes organizations that have become demoralized, have lost faith in their leadership, or are otherwise suffering serious failures in the integrating forces. These circumstances tend to create an "every department for itself" mentality, with each unit scurrying to find allies and to protect its turf. When the organization has been divisionalized, with each division enjoying great autonomy, division chiefs may begin to believe that they need to protect their operations from the overall chaos—which means that they may reduce to virtually nothing their efforts to support the overall organization.

Internal differentiation and competition also has a significant impact when organizations—even very healthy ones—attempt to change. Any meaningful change will almost certainly strengthen some internal units at the expense of others. Those that will be strengthened are typically proponents of the change. Those that will be weakened seldom are.

Two separate but related trends during the 1980s and early 1990s illustrate this clearly: the total quality management (TQM) movement and the emphasis on customer satisfaction. Total quality management proposed to move the responsibility for quality away from the staff quality office and into the manufacturing department. It also stressed that designs should be frozen once they were handed over to manufacturing. Both these changes tended to strengthen manufacturing vis-à-vis other units. In the process, however, TQM also proposed to move meaningful responsibilities away from supervisors and into work units. While supervisors didn't constitute a separate unit, they were an identifiable group, a group that now saw itself as losing authority and power. Thus TQM created at least two major stresses in organizations, and in many companies the success of its implementation was determined only after some significant internal power struggles.

The emphasis on quality as customer satisfaction was related to but not simply a product of the quality movement. This emphasis created fundamental problems for many companies, particularly in high-tech fields, that had identified quality as technical excellence. When quality is technical excellence, the engineers are clearly in control. When quality becomes customer satisfaction, though, the engineering function can quickly find itself subordinate to the marketing operation. This struggle dominated the internal histories of numerous high-tech companies, and for many of them it's still not a settled issue. Interestingly, IBM's recent history was almost the reverse. The company had been dominated by its emphasis on marketing and service; low-cost manufacturing had never been a goal of the old IBM. Suddenly, however, price became a major factor in the personal computer market, which meant that manufacturing suddenly assumed an importance it never had before.

Internal differentiation and competition has a third implication for organizations and organizational change. Chapter 4 stressed that all purposes are ultimately individual purposes. There can never be such a thing as an organizational purpose that exists independently of the individuals who comprise the organization. But the majority of these individuals do not identify first with the organization; rather, they identify with the unit or subunit to which they belong. Thus their individual purposes tend to be far more closely related to the purposes of their immediate units than to those of the organization at large.

Organizations have dealt with this problem at the senior management and executive level for decades. Managers typically develop through one of the organizational stovepipes, and some stovepipes lead far more reliably to the front office than do others. At GM, every manager through Roger Smith has come up through the financial function. At Hewlett-Packard, on the other hand, CEOs have traditionally been technical people. And few if any organizations are headed by individuals who rose through the ranks in purchasing or human resources management. All this despite the attempts of almost every major organization to provide rising executives with a variety of managerial experience.

The result? Virtually everyone in the organization, from the shop floor to the front office, sees the organization from a viewpoint first developed through apprenticeship in a very specific function. Does this mean that the individual adopts the purposes of the unit? No. His or her purposes are still individual, but these purposes are more closely related to those of the immediate organizational unit than to those of the organization as a whole. In organizations as in nature, purposes are normally local and seldom global.

All this relates to attempts at organizational change in yet another way. As I write this, Jack Welch of GE remains one of the most highly respected CEOs in the country. When *Business Week* runs a story based on comments by Mr. Welch, the headline is most apt to read "GE plans to. . . ." Is this how a worker in GE's jet engine operation or a senior manager in its financial arm is likely to interpret the story? Seldom. Instead, these individuals, and most of those in the organization, see the statement as something made by an individual. Their first response will most likely be not "Oh, we're now going in a new direction" but "How do you think what Welch wants to do will affect us?" And if the organization's new direction appears harmful to the individual's immediate unit, he or she may very well begin working to blunt or modify Mr. Welch's stated intentions.

In short, however we may look at an organization from outside, it is very, very difficult to find "the voice of the organization" once you are inside.

Now we have identified yet another reason why organizations are reluctant to change: the differential impact of almost all changes on internal units. Organizations without strong centers easily devolve into feuding internal centers of power. Whenever an organization proposes to change, it enhances the operation of some of these centers and diminishes the operation of others, thus creating or fueling power struggles among these parts. Then, because all purposes are individual purposes and generally local, individuals are more apt to identify their purposes with their immediate organizational units than with the organization as a whole.

These factors constitute a powerful constituency for the status quo. We should marvel not that serious organizational change fails so often but that it does at times really succeed.

These factors are also what we would expect from the basic principles inherent in evolution and thus in all significant change. Evolution amply illustrates that change is inherently unpredictable and unplanned and can occur only in individuals. Thousands of species have vanished because they overadapted to niches that changed or vanished. Organisms with complex internal structures are far more resistant to environmental pressures than simpler organisms are. In large part, this is because the relationships among the components of these structures tend to drive the organization more than do external events.

So much resistance to change! Yet we know that successful change—evolution—does occur in the natural world. Perhaps our problems with organizational change are not with change itself but with a faulty understanding of how successful change occurs. Perhaps a deeper look at the principles underlying evolutionary change might help us organize so that our companies could change more successfully.

The rest of the book attempts to do just that. All the conclusions reached in the first five chapters have been based on the assumption that an organization seeks equilibrium, the lowest energy state that will permit the organization to achieve its goals. We are stuck with these conclusions only if organizations are equilibrium-seeking systems. Fortunately, not all systems seek equilibrium. Scientists in the past two decades or so have discovered a different kind of system—a complex, adaptive system. They have discovered that these systems may be responsible for much of evolution. And their discoveries suggest ways in which organizations can change continually and successfully to stay in sync with their environments.

We now leave the safe, predictable world of equilibrium-seeking systems and turn to far-from-equilibrium, complex adaptive systems. First, though, lets draw some lessons from the role of internal structure in biological and organizational evolution.

Internal Structure: The Lessons

Neither organisms nor organizations evolve quickly and easily, and their internal structures exert a powerful influence on how they can evolve. Here are a few lessons we might draw from this knowledge:

- The more dependent your organization is on technology, the more it will be tied to that technology—and the harder it will be for it to adopt new and different technologies. Whenever you do adopt a new technology, ask yourself in advance how it might handicap you in the future. Technology is *always* less flexible than people.

▪ If your organization has been relatively stable and has not pursued continuous process improvement (CPI) or business process redesign (BPR), your processes are somewhere between relatively and embarrassingly inefficient. Either CPI or BPR will probably yield useful results if you give them the time and attention they need (which is quite a lot). Be warned, though: If you begin either program and follow through on it, you will find that you need to change both organizational functions and structures as well as processes.

▪ Do you know what the incentives are in your organization? No, not just the formal pay plan and bonus system. The *other* incentives: What gets individuals promoted? What gets them into trouble? What keeps them out of trouble? Why should anyone bother to do more than a satisfactory job? What's the organizational ratio between "Attaboys" and "Awhells"? (In an effective organization individuals are praised again and again for every time they receive criticism; in most organizations, it's just the reverse.) You may be amazed to find what the real incentives are.

▪ How well do you understand your organization's fundamental competencies? This may sound like an easy question; it is not. For example, even in a traditional, functional organization, there are tremendous differences among individual workers and managements in how well they deal with their peers. In some organizations, this kind of coordination seldom happens effectively. In others, individuals do it consistently quite well. While the difference is cultural, the ability to communicate effectively sideways is a clear and important competence.

▪ How often do workers and managers in your organization get useful feedback? Even in a traditional organization, effective feedback enables everyone to do a better job. And if you intend for members of your organization to be even a little bit self-organized, you must provide them with effective feedback systems. *Individuals cannot control their performance unless they receive prompt, specific, direct feedback.* Who knows? You might be able to transform your organization significantly if you did nothing more than ensure that everyone got this kind of feedback.

• Books on management often speak as though "lower-level" (nonmanagement) employees constitute the single greatest obstacle to change. This is nice mythology, but poor fact. If you want to create significant change in your organization, you are at least as likely to find that the major obstacle isn't workers but supervisors and managers. Managers have typically spent years in their function and have worked hard to reach a position of power and status within it. Unless they believe that a proposed change will increase or at a minimum preserve this power and status, they have adequate reason to oppose it.

• Whenever you're contemplating significant change, take the time necessary to ask how it affects *each* subordinate unit. It will strengthen the status and power of some, reduce that of others. The crucial question for the change, then, is what to do about those who will see the change as a threat. Answer this question before you attempt any meaningful change.

• Once again, despite all the complexities aided by an organization's component subsystems and internal units, only individuals can change. All change is hostage to the question: Why would this individual want to do this instead of what he or she is doing now? Answer it effectively, or else.

6

Coevolve or Perish

Have you perhaps thought that evolution was a simple matter of the "survival of the fittest," in which the best organisms survived and the rest perished? Not in the real world. Organisms survive as part of a constantly evolving environment composed of species, their prey, their competitors, their predators, and everything else that affects them. Does this sound like the competitive environment you know?

The Reality of Coevolution

We commonly speak of the evolution of species as though it were an isolated event. Horses evolved from extremely small animals to their present-day form. Cells evolved from extremely simple bacteria to the complex organisms that make up human beings. And present-day *Homo sapiens* evolved from earlier forms of humans, which in turn evolved from lower mammals. And dolphins apparently evolved from land-dwelling rather than sea-dwelling ancestors.

In one sense, all this is true. In another, more important sense, it is not. No species ever evolved in a vacuum. Instead, all biological organisms *coevolve*. The difference matters—greatly.

Species coevolve in a dual sense. They coevolve with their environments—or they become extinct. And they coevolve with that specific part of their environment comprised of other species that are their competitors, their prey, or their predators—or they become extinct. This never-ending dance constitutes the heart of evolution.

Picture one of the great cats a few million years ago. Perhaps the grassland in which the cat hunts becomes gradually colder. Clearly, any cat offspring that have a warmer coat or some other mutation that fits the colder climate will have a survival advantage. This may remain only a change within the species. If enough of these mutations occur, however, a new species comes into being. Because this species has a series of advantages over the existing one, it may replace it. The original species has coevolved with its environment into a new species.

That merely begins our hypothetical coevolutionary tale. Let us suppose that the great cat's prey is an ancestor of a current antelope. The cat runs faster than the antelope, so once it can spot one it can catch it and turn it into supper. Then a mutation occurs in the antelope that makes the animal more difficult to see; perhaps its color changes just enough to permit it to blend in with the tall grass in a more effective way. The cats have more difficulty finding food, and their numbers diminish significantly. But then a mutation makes the cat's eye more sensitive to fine gradations in color; now it can spot an antelope more quickly. The mutation passes on through generations, either modifying the existing species or forming a new species.

To change the metaphor from a few paragraphs above, all evolution occurs within the great web of life. A change anywhere in the web affects potentially every other point in the web—and usually in unpredictable ways. Each individual species within the web changes constantly, searching for some advantage over the other species with which it must compete and for some additional protection from its predators. What seems an insurmountable evolutionary advance at one point in the web may become a liability as other species change to counteract that advance. And any species unlucky enough to stand still while others are evolving will most likely find itself a footnote in some textbook on fossils.

Does that perhaps sound like the competitive situation your organization must cope with in the late 1990s?

Why Coevolution Matters

Planned organizational change all too often assumes stability and predictability, but the world is busy coevolving around the organization in very predictable ways. Organizations may even plan to evolve, but the success of their changes requires that they effectively coevolve with the other players in a highly uncertain environment.

As I write this, no market presents a clearer picture of coevolution in action than does home entertainment. In the mid-1990s, these are a few of the major players:

- The makers of dedicated game-playing machines: Nintendo, Sega, and their competitors.
- The makers of personal computers, who have been modifying their machines into more effective platforms for games and other entertainment.
- Cable TV companies, seeking to find ways to make the family TV set and its cable connections an interactive entertainment machine.
- Satellite companies, purveying much the same fare as cable companies, but seeking a competitive advantage in greater bandwidth and more channels.
- The companies that create games. As we who play the games know, the competition for the newest and most challenging game grows more intense every day.

Would you attempt to predict the outcome of the competition among these players? If you are a player, would you attempt to make a single competitive move without considering what the responding moves of the other players might be? Or of other competitors not on the list but still competing for home entertainment dollars: home theater; TV; radio; low-, medium-, and high-end stereo systems; and such low-tech endeavors as board games?

Even relatively established markets feature coevolution, though at a slower pace. Goldstar moved a step ahead in its Korean market by introducing a refrigerator able to keep *kim chi* edible longer than any of its competitors. Mail order vendors of fancy papers, such as Paper Direct and On Paper, constantly upgrade their products in an attempt to gain a few months lead on their competitors with a new idea, at the same time that they try to prevent these same competitors from getting a similar lead on them.

You may be familiar with a form of game theory based on "the prisoner's dilemma" that underscores the importance of coevolution—though of a very limited form of coevolution. Its moves are based on the assumption that the important factors are known or predictable, while in biological coevolution, they never are. In fact, the greatest gain comes precisely from coming up with a move that competitors cannot anticipate or respond to quickly. However, game theory does recognize that no move can ever be taken without considering the potential responding moves. To that extent, it mirrors the reality of coevolution.[1]

These changes aren't occurring just in the external environment. Every organization is also constantly changing and coevolving internally as its internal units struggle to achieve their goals, often in competition with one another.

Some struggles might have no clear effects on the viability of the company except perhaps to divert attention that should be spent on dealing with the external environment. Other internal struggles might have a clearer impact on the organization's competitive strength. For instance, the sales department of one division might evolve over time to the point where it became the single sales organization for all the company's divisions. Then if the company needed to decentralize sales, to give greater autonomy to the different product divisions so as to bring them "closer to the customer," it might find itself unable to do so because of the sheer power concentrated in the sales department.

In other words, the coevolution of an organization's internal units significantly affects how it can respond to the competitive challenges in its environment—that is, its own ability to coevolve in its environment.

Because all evolution is coevolution, coevolution never ceases either in nature or in organizations. It may occur with dramatic rapidity, as the major players in the American automobile market coevolved from the late 1970s to the mid-1990s. Or it may occur far more slowly, as when the different home builders in an established market gradually change their offerings to respond to home-buyer tastes and the moves of their competitors.

And long periods of highly stable, very slow evolution may be succeeded by brief, dramatic periods of rapid coevolution. However it occurs, though, coevolution never ceases.

That last statement needs to be modified slightly. When a company is awake and aware, coevolution never ceases. (Every major CEO I know of who has led a major change effort has said that the change is never-ending.) When it preoccupies itself with defending its present position, looking inward, and spending its energy on internal competitive struggles, however, it can indeed cease to coevolve, because it fails to notice what it needs to be coevolving with. Coevolution happens when, and only when, an organism or an organization receives and uses a constant information flow from its environment. In other words:

> *An organization coevolves successfully vis à vis its competitors only when it constantly seeks, gets, and uses new ideas and data from its environment.*

Supertransformational Change?

Unfortunately, when organizations operate as stable, equilibrium-seeking systems, they accept into their information flow only the facts and ideas that confirm their current structure. That produces a stalemate in which organizational change becomes increasingly difficult and often occurs only in a traumatic attempt to prevent the organization's extinction. To function as an adaptive system, an organization must change its fundamental approach to information. To do this, in turn, it must change the very basis on which the organization operates. It must open itself up broadly to the impact of its environment.

What happens when it does this? It gets shaken from its janitorial closets to its executive washrooms. In the words of the poem, "Nothing is ever the same again." Nothing is ever the same again because the organization deliberately creates porous boundaries to replace the airtight boundaries it depended on to maintain the integrity of its structure. It becomes consciously dependent on suppliers, customers, and the environment at large in a way it has never experienced before. In just a few words, it gives up effective control in return for effective adaptation.

This constitutes an enormous change for the organization, at least as great as any cultural or transformational change could be. How great?

This means that it gives up any attempt to seriously predict its future. "Strategic planning" becomes a series of projections, made on the assumption that they will be constantly tested against reality and constantly changed. It develops the ability of its components to self-organize. Self-organization is the basis of much evolution and all human action, and an organization that can effectively implement self-organization at the unit and individual level can take a giant stride toward effective coevolution. It converts as many internal units as possible into quasi-autonomous, profit-making organizations by adopting the basic strengths of free enterprise within its boundaries. It can accomplish all this only by keeping its boundaries, internal and external, open to new ideas and facts *and* by developing the competence necessary to evaluate, develop, and implement new strategies based on these ideas and facts.

Does all this sound daunting? It should. However, the remainder of this chapter and the rest of the book will provide you with concrete ways to test and implement these ideas yourself. Changing from an equilibrium-seeking, locked-into-its-current-form organization to an adaptive, complex organization that (in Peter Senge's phrase) continually creates its future can never be easy. These chapters, however, will show you how to make the change effectively and without unnecessary trauma.

Kick-Starting the Information Flow

Because ideas and data that are at odds with its current state might threaten the organization's integrity, the organization has a powerful motivation to reject them. The first and most basic problem for any organization that intends to coevolve successfully is how to refocus itself so that it can accept and use this disconfirming information and new ideas.

As is the case with biological organisms, the environment

always includes the organization's competitors. But it is never limited to them. It also includes suppliers, stockholders, government regulators, the state of the economy and—more than anything else—its customers.

A Brief Reality Check

How well do you know your customers? Lean back in your arm chair and answer these three questions:

1. Precisely how do your customers use your product or service? Exactly what benefit do they get from it?
2. What percentage of your customers buy from you repeatedly? What percentage buy regularly from you and also from one or more of your competitors?
3. Why do the people who aren't your customers buy from your competitors instead of from you?

You should know the answers to at least one or two of these questions. If you don't, you're lacking important information. If you don't know the answer to any of the questions, you're inviting a competitor to move in and take over your business.

Information From Your Customers

No organization can coevolve successfully without knowing its customers—and furthermore knowing them better than any of its competitors do. Knowing them won't make your organization an adaptive organization, but it's a necessary ingredient. Besides, focusing on customers is productive enough that you'll never get into serious trouble by emphasizing it.

Okay, everyone agrees that you should focus on customers. Now, what information do you need from and about them? Here are some questions you need answers to:

• What characteristics of your products or services are most important to them?

- How well does your company rank on these characteristics compared to:

> —Your customers' absolute preferences (in other words, how close do you come to satisfying your customer completely)?
> —Your performance a year ago?
> —Your competitors' performance?

These questions are more or less standard. Three others are often overlooked, but play an even greater part in providing your company with information it needs to evolve and adapt:

1. Why do the people who aren't your customers or who used to be your customers deal with your competitors instead of with you? If you're a retail business, hire someone to stand outside your competitors' places of business and ask customers why they shop there. If you have a relatively small number of customers, hire a firm to interview those who've left you to find out why. Or think up another way. Be innovative. Just learn why people don't deal with you.

2. What are the pressing issues for your customers? Not their wants, but their make-or-break business concerns. If you have few customers and provide them with highly customized products and/or services, make sure that someone asks them. And asks them regularly. If you supply a large market and have too many customers to talk with individually, find a way to survey them, do sample interviews and focus groups, whatever you need to do to get a feel for their world and what's happening in it.

3. How do your most progressive and innovative customers see the world? Where do they believe they're headed? How do they believe their business is changing? Will it change in the next five years? Your most innovative customers are one of the best sources of ideas for new products and services, even for new markets, you will ever find.

So after you start getting this data, what happens then? Some of the data won't sound good. Your products or services aren't as good as they used to be or as good as your competitors'. Your planning is taking you in a direction different from that of your most innovative customers. Almost everyone's first reaction will be a form of denial: What do they know? Ours is better than theirs and we can prove it! We've already planned the logical way for us to expand our offerings; besides, they're just a small sample—what do they know? And so on and on.

Your organization has just encountered the first test of its resolve. Are you going to slough off the comments that don't fit your preconceptions? If so, you're struggling to reject disconfirming information and to maintain the existing system. No openness to adaptation there. Or are you going to start the painful process of evaluating the information and then evaluating your goals in the light of the information you're receiving? You'll probably find that you're much less sure of the direction you should be traveling. Congratulations. Every additional bit of uncertainty you can tolerate takes you that much closer to your goal of successful coevolution with your environment.

Information About Your Competitors

A Brief Reality Check

Answer these three questions:

1. Exactly who are your competitors?
2. How does your company differentiate itself from each of these competitors? Specifically, what do you offer that your competitors don't?
3. What will most likely be the next move of your most important competitor?

If you don't know the answer to one or more of these questions, your company lacks the information it requires to coevolve successfully in its competitive environment.

You should know the apparent strategy, competitive advantage, products and/or services of at least your major competitors as intimately as they do. You probably know how to do this better than I do, but here are a few suggestions you might not have considered:

- Do you and your competitors have help, service, or customer support activities? Find a half-dozen or dozen individuals whose objectivity you trust and have each of them make a call to your activity and to your competitors' activities. We know that most customers value service highly. How does yours compare with that of your competitors?

- Are your employees required to use your products or services? If so, what would happen if they had a free choice? Would they still choose yours, or would they prefer those of a competitor? You might want to give them a choice and see what happens. Or you might be able to stimulate it (for example, by having the purchasing department evaluate your products and those of your competitors using its standard methodology). Insisting that your employees use your products or services often makes good business sense. On the other hand, it can easily blind you to real advantages that your competitors' offerings have.

- You do purchase every product or service your competitors produce and then analyze it carefully, don't you? But are the people who do the analysis paid to be objective, and do they get heard when they come up with bad news? (Remember Mr. Ricard at GM. He presented extremely valuable intelligence on the set-up time of one of GM's key competitors and for his trouble was called a liar and pointedly ignored.)

- Finally, do key people in your organization belong to all the relevant associations for your industry? Do they read the publications carefully, listen to the presentations carefully, and network carefully? Do they also belong to key customer and supplier associations and listen just as carefully there?

Once you begin using all this information, you may find yourself caught between two poles. On the one hand, you will be tempted to match your competitors; if they produce a new carbon-fiber widget or all-in-one financial account, shouldn't you produce one as well? On the other hand, you have your own strategy, based on a clear view (you hope) of your competitive advantage; shouldn't you follow it? Effective coevolution requires that you live constantly in this tension.

You can follow one principle, one that most biological organisms follow unthinkingly: Concentrate on providing the benefits that your competitors cannot quickly or easily match. A few companies understand how to hold costs to an absolute minimum, and then keep reducing them. Letting yourself get caught in a price war with one of them, which is often the quick and easy solution, will almost certainly be painful, if not fatal.

This leads to a final thought. When you know your competitors intimately, you won't be constantly surprised by their competitive moves. Whatever else, being able to anticipate them gives you planning time, so that your response flows out of your own competitive strategy, not from a knee-jerk response to their moves.

Information About Stockholders, Governments, Communities, and Others

Organizations require information on these aspects of their environment as much as they do information on customers and competitors. Unfortunately, their efforts to get such information are often handicapped by their fundamental orientation to these groups: "educating" them. Educate stockholders on the fundamental value of the stock. Educate legislators and regulators on the virtue of a pro-business point of view. Educate the community on the value of the company and the virtue of providing it with favorable tax treatment.

Companies engage in these "educational" activities constantly, as they should. But when you're busy "educating," you often fail to listen properly. Instead of listening to stockholder complaints, the company explains why the complaints are wrong. Instead of listening to the force behind legislators' and regulators' actions, the company explains why they ought not to think that way. Instead of listening to the community's concerns over the durability of the company's jobs, it explains why they ought not to be concerned. In every such situation, educating without carefully listening moves the organization one more step away from understanding and coevolving effectively with its environment.

Listening With Every Ear, Thinking With Every Brain

Instead of offering specific suggestions on how you might listen effectively to these parts of your organization's environment, it might be more helpful to you if I stressed two closely related points that are critical to listening to any source outside the organization. First, the organization needs for every one of its members to listen to its environment, and then it needs to listen to all their reports. Second, the organization needs to become very sophisticated at identifying the most useful information and then in using it.

Traditional, equilibrium-seeking organizations attempt to maintain their equilibrium, despite changes in their environment, by sharply limiting both the units authorized to collect data and the kind of data they collect. Typically, they organize the marketing function and perhaps the public relations function to collect information. Typically, the data they are to collect are spelled out in some detail, and the functions make little attempt to collect data outside these limits. When an entrepreneurial marketing or PR manager goes in search of other data, she will likely find that the organization has no interest in hearing about it.

How do you change this? Over the past decade, a number of companies have gotten excellent results by sending their workers regularly to visit their customers and then by listening to the workers when they returned. That's a good place to start, but don't send people to visit customers until the organization makes a clear commitment to listen to them when they return. Then begin with the customers most receptive to the visits and expand from there. Once this builds momentum, see that your sales force becomes another source of competitive intelligence.

And your managers and executives should be bringing back more intelligence from community, industry, and management meetings. (Beware of the latter, however. Executives and managers are exceptionally good at persuading each other that they're all on the right track, or selling the newest fad as the cure-all. Don't forget the executive who toured the United States in 1936 and returned to confidently predict that Roosevelt would never be elected to a second term.) Keep in mind that status is not a reliable guide to accuracy.

Because they so severely limit the scope of the data they receive from outside their boundaries, traditional organizations have very primitive methods for evaluating data outside "normal channels." If you intend for your organization to coevolve successfully, you must become more sophisticated in this area—and quickly.

How? Unfortunately, answers are hard to find, because so few organizations have attempted to find them. If the information flows up the normal chain of command, every layer provides the opportunity to say "no," without being able to say "yes." If it bypasses the chain of command, most managers look on it as an aberration and a threat to their authority. Later chapters have some very specific suggestions for organizing that will help resolve this dilemma. For now, begin by making your interest in "unauthorized" information clear. Don't just write a letter; your managers and workers know they don't need to pay attention if your only investment is a pro forma letter. Talk it up. Make it an item of personal interest to you. Ask your direct reports what they've learned; if they've learned nothing, tell them to go learn. If you possibly can, ask the frontline people what they've learned. Remember, you're changing a deeply ingrained pattern.

One last note. Accept the data you get. This doesn't mean you agree with it or approve it. That comes later. But don't ever respond with a version of "Yeah, I understand—but we already considered that and it doesn't really matter." Listen, ask intelligent questions, and take notes. If the data aren't useful, there's plenty of time to decide that. And if you don't reject it up front, you may well find that there's something there that hasn't been adequately considered before.

Moving the Information Through the Organization

Here we can only begin to talk about moving information through the organization. Because all effective change (and effective stability, too) depends on information, the remaining chapters of the book will deal with it again and again. But we need to begin here, because once an organization can get data from its environment it must effectively evaluate and use that data—or its entire data-gathering effort has been wasted. So information must move freely through the organization—which it doesn't do in most organizations today—and then it must be evaluated seriously, effectively, and efficiently.

We might begin by looking at a lesson that intelligence organizations (such as the CIA) have learned over the years. Seldom will you get a nice, neat package of information that tells you what your competitors are doing, in what direction your market is moving, what key contributors may be leaving you, or how stockholders will react to your operation over the next year. Instead, it comes in driblets, a piece of information here, an apparently unrelated piece there. Then a bit of information appears that suddenly enables you to begin to make sense of these pieces. But, just as in working a jigsaw puzzle, you can't see the whole pattern unless you have all the individual pieces that make it up.

Traditional organizations generally lack the ability to do this. Their managers and executives expect information to come in carefully packaged wholes, complete with executive summaries. If you want someone's evaluation of the progress of distance education over the next five years, that may work. But if you want to know how your market is changing or what your competitors are up to, it almost certainly will not. To get that information, particularly when it's unexpected, you have to develop the ability to gather and then remember lots of bits and pieces. If you don't have a formal intelligence unit within the organization, you might consider establishing one (under whatever name seems best.) It's useless to try to do strategic planning unless it's based on careful, competent, strategic intelligence.

But getting and using information from outside just begins attacking the problem of how to move information generally through the organization. Just as executives and managers in traditional organizations expect information to be neatly packaged, so they take a very restrictive view of information: No one should have it unless they specifically need it to do their job. Is the organization in danger of losing market share and thus of having a reduction in force? This is the business of no one but top management. Is the chief of purchasing having an affair with the chief of finance? That is no one's business at all—except perhaps for the CEO, who is their mutual supervisor.

No one who has worked in an organization ever believed this for a moment. If the organization is in danger of having a reduction in force, no other information is even remotely as important—not today's production goals, not the mission of the company, not anything. And the relationship between the chief of purchasing and the chief of finance, besides its titilation value, might also indicate who is going into this year's budget fight a few yards ahead of everyone else.

A Brief Reality Check

Think objectively about your organization and your need for information. Specifically, think about the three most important facts or rumors that you've heard in the past month or so. How many of them did you hear through an official channel—staff meetings, official letters, the company newsletter? And how many of them did you hear from a friend or colleague through the grapevine. Now, how many others do you suppose heard this important information through the same grapevine rather than through official channels?

This is a fact: Individuals are interested in whatever information will affect them as individuals. The difference between news that has little to do with them and news that affects them personally constitutes precisely the difference between data and information. If humans are a product of the evolutionary process, and if organizations form the environment in which they thrive or perish, what else would you expect? That they need not worry because the organization will take care of them? Neither managers nor workers believe that as we approach the beginning of the twenty-first century. Organizations that intend to provide all their contributors with the information they need to make intelligent decisions will be far more successful.

This is another fact: When the official channels provide information that individuals need, the grapevine largely dries up. Surprising as it may sound, people would prefer to get their information through official sources than through unofficial ones. Learn from that. Your company organ can't print the current status of the relationship between the chief of purchasing and the chief of finance—though that would assure it a far wider readership than it now has. But it can print realistic information about the company's situation, so that managers and workers alike come to believe they can depend on it for the information they need.

Jack Stack and SRC are perhaps the most famous example of how information openness can transform a company. When he bought the nearly bankrupt operation from what was then International Harvester, it was a shaky deal at best. In its first year, 1984, SRC lost $61,000. Nine years later, it earned a 6 percent return on sales that were six times as great. Why? At least in part because Stack not only makes information on SRC's operations available to every contributor, but also provides regular training to everyone in how to interpret this information. As a result, every contributor knows just what's happening to the company and what he or she can do to help it happen better.[2]

So this is the first guideline on information within the company: Give individuals the information they need to make intelligent decisions about their jobs, their results, and their careers. Don't make a distinction. Give them everything they need not only to perform successfully but also to conduct their lives successfully.

For instance, do you have E-mail in your organization? Yes? Then you can be sure that every bit of remotely relevant information is already passing from individual to individual at the speed of electrons. *Don't* try to control it. *Do* wire yourself into it. Make your E-mail address available to everyone in the organization (and to suppliers and customers as well). Read and answer your E-mail. It is *not* simply paper mail by a different, slightly faster method. It is a truly new way of communicating.

And Now, a Word About "Survival of the Fittest"

Here you are, over halfway through a book on organizational evolution, and you haven't encountered anything about one of the most venerable evolutionary concepts: survival of the fittest. Why?

The general answer is this: "Survival of the fittest" is a great polemic, a great slogan, but a virtually useless concept. Here's why:

- If "survival of the fittest" truly meant anything, it would enable us to predict which organisms or organizations would survive. No biologist would ever use it this way. Why? Because, as this chapter has stressed, all evolution is coevolution. The word *fittest* has no meaning apart from a specific environment. In the last century, a whole theory of economics built on evolutionary theory grew up, proclaiming that the best economic policy was pure laissez-faire—leave business completely alone and let the fittest survive. That approach defined *fittest* in terms of an environment in which the federal and state governments were nonplayers. This constitutes one option. In the present, governments are extremely active in the economic sphere. Consider, for instance, the impact of EPA, OSHA, ADA, and affirmative action regulations. Their presence creates an entirely different environment. Companies that might have been "fittest" if there were no government presence might well become extinct in an environment in which governments are major players. Which is really "fittest"? There's no answer, because all evolution is coevolution, so all evolution depends on the environment in which it occurs.

- In fact, *fittest* has no predictive value whatsoever. It is a self-defining, backward-looking concept. Who survives? The fittest. How do you know they were the fittest? Because they survived.

- Finally, "survival of the fittest" tells us nothing about evolution itself. It says that, given a specific environment and a specific balance of species, some will survive and others won't. In organizational terms, it says that given a specific competitive environment and a specific set of companies, some will survive and others won't. It doesn't even consider the fact that one or more of these companies will evolve to a different way of doing business so that they completely redefine what *fittest* means. In 1992, Compaq was in serious trouble. It did not appear to be the "fittest" in any sense. So what did the company do? It mutated (changed) and attacked the market in a very different way. By early 1995, Compaq was the world's leading producer of personal computers. It became the "fittest" by evolving out of a situation in which it was becoming an also-ran.

The moral? Don't waste your time worrying about the "survival of the fittest." It will happen, simply because we define the fittest as those who survive. Concentrate instead on responding to your competitive environment and coevolving successfully with it. Then, by definition, you will be among the fittest. (Some things in life truly are simple.)

7

For Competitive Success, Surprise Is Worth More Than Predictability

No one can successfully predict the course of biological coevolution. And no one can successfully predict the course of organizational coevolution. The conclusion: For competitive success in a dynamic world, surprise is worth more than predictability.

When scientists look back on evolution, they see patterns of development from one species to another. Could they have predicted the development if they had been in the past looking forward? No. Biological evolution has never followed a neat, predictable path. Stephen Jay Gould, a paleontologist who has had a major impact on modern interpretations of biological evolution, has made this assessment of the unpredictability of evolution:

> [Evolutionary] history can be explained, with satisfying rigor if evidence be adequate, after a sequence of events unfolds, but it cannot be predicted with any precision beforehand. . . . History includes too much chaos, or

extremely sensitive dependence on minute and unmea-
surable differences in initial conditions, leading to
massively divergent outcomes based on tiny and un-
knowable disparities in starting points. And history includes too much contingency, or shaping of present
results by long chains of unpredictable antecedent
states, rather than immediate determination by timeless laws of nature.[1]

In other words, the future remains just as unpredictable at
the biological level as it is at the organizational level. If Gould
had been writing about organizations, however, he might have
added this sentence:

Where organizational evolution is concerned, the unpredictable part of the future is more valuable for successful competitive coevolution than what can be
predicted.

Why should this be true? Simple. Almost every company
can deal effectively with the conditions it successfully predicts.
If Acme Widget plans on a market for its products that will grow
8 percent per year for the next five years, and the market does
so, Acme has positioned itself to deal with the increase. Unfortunately, so has each of Acme's competitors. If we all predict the
same basic future and it happens, we're all passengers in the
same boat. No one has a significant advantage over the others.

But what if the unexpected happens? Everyone's plans are
tossed awry, but the company or companies that can respond
most rapidly and effectively to surprise will have a competitive
edge. No one anticipated the celebrated double murder that O. J.
Simpson was tried for, but once it happened a few publishers
were able to get books on the newsstands in a matter of weeks
and reap profits from the event's notoriety. The ability to anticipate developments in telecommunications no doubt has value.
The ability to respond quickly to developments that weren't anticipated has even more value—because it can create a meaningful competitive advantage.

Surprise! It's Post-it Notes

Don't expect to find all the surprise and unpredictability ema-
nating from outside the company. In a highly dynamic environment like that at the end of the twentieth century, what happens
inside a company is equally unforeseeable. Ask CEOs such as
Paul Allaire (Xerox) or Lewis Platt (Hewlett-Packard) what their
highly successful companies will look like in five years. The answer you're most likely to get is: Different, but we don't know
just how. Companies such as these or GE or Motorola that have
committed themselves to successful coevolution with their markets know that change and unpredictability will be constants.

Unpredictability runs even deeper. Certainly the most famous and most successful new product of the 1980s was the
3M company's Post-it Notes™. First of all, no one would have
predicted the product; it didn't fit any established category of
office supplies. And what a brilliant job 3M did in planning and
marketing the product! Certainly they were massively successful
with Post-it Notes—but consider the following:

- The individual who came up with the idea wasn't involved in product research and didn't work in the division
  that developed the product.
- The just-tacky-enough adhesive that makes the product
  work began life as a failed adhesive.
- The market test of the product proved unsuccessful.
- When 3M finally released the product, the company mis-
  understood both what the real market was and how extensive it would be.

Would any other major company in America have gotten
through this series of events and actually launched the product?
Possibly, but none of them spring to mind. The fact is that 3M
may be the best large company in the world at turning unexpected and uninvited ideas into profitable products.

In short, what separates winners from losers in a highly dynamic market is not so much excellence at planning as excellence
in adapting to and profiting from unexpected events—both inside and outside the company. This shouldn't surprise us since

the successful evolution of mammals and ultimately of human beings was made possible by an unpredictable and still heatedly debated event: the extinction of dinosaurs. It's unlikely that mammals could ever have competed with dinosaurs, but once the dinosaurs exited mammals were positioned to move to the center of the evolutionary stage.

Technology: A Basic Engine of Unpredictability

Should we say "The future is unpredictable" and just wait for an unpredictable change to occur before we respond? Not necessarily. The future will always surprise us, but we can make a few educated guesses about the cause of some of these surprises. You already know that you need to look at what's happening with your customers, competitors, suppliers, government legislators and regulators, and other aspects of your competitive environment. This chapter looks at an increasing source of surprise: technology. And it looks at three different ways in which technology can produce surprise: the technology itself; the impact of the technology on organizations; and the coevolution of organizations with technology.

Keeping Up With Technology

Every organization that wants to deal effectively with the unexpected knows it must look constantly and closely at developments in technology around it. It must remain technologically up to date and it must monitor its competitors' and customers' attempts to do so. It also needs to keep a weather eye on technology that is emerging *outside* its current markets and competitors.

- Earlier, we looked at the frantic race for success in the home-entertainment market. Because of the variety of competitors and technologies, no one can predict the winning technology or technologies. And there may be no winner until an unexpected shift gives a clear advantage to one technology or another.

▪ Changes in manufacturing often get overlooked in our preoccupation with the impact of computers and communications on office work. Even staid manufacturing industries, however, are applying new technology at an accelerating pace. Computer-assisted design (CAD) and computer-assisted manufacturing (CAM) used to require horrendously powerful mainframes, which were found in only a few large companies. Today? The surprising development of the personal computer means that organizations with a few desktop computers or workstations can routinely use CAD. CAM has been succeeded by CIM (computer-integrated manufacturing), and any organization large enough to have a significant manufacturing operation can easily afford CIM and the computers that run it.

▪ A decade ago, most companies were focusing their computers on accounting, inventory, and other traditional internal functions. Not American Hospital Supply, which took a very surprising path. It put computer terminals in its customers' operations. Believing that if you can't beat 'em, buy 'em, Baxter Corporation bought AHS and poured time, effort, and money into the system it had created. Now, Baxter has terminals not just in its customer hospitals but throughout these hospitals. Supplies are delivered to where they're needed, and Baxter claims to maintain a 99.3 percent order rate.

The Impact of Technology on Organizations

Technology by itself exerts a powerful and often unanticipated force for change, but the impact it has on organizations is even more significant.

▪ A number of individuals predicted the success of E-Mail, but few understood the impact it would have on organizations. People communicate differently when they use E-mail than when they use letter mail. More important, as Chapter 6 pointed out, they communicate much more widely, much more frequently, and about a much wider range of topics. The information that moves through E-mail is inherently uncontrollable, particularly now that more and more companies are hooked into the Internet. But we still don't know what the ultimate impact of everyone being able to communicate with everyone else will be.

A Brief Reality Check

Picture this situation. News reporters have discovered that they can use E-mail to bypass the organization's formal channels and ask individual workers and managers directly for information and opinions. Visualize yourself as the CEO of a company that is throwing all its resources into developing a new product to save itself from bankruptcy or takeover. You know that all your key people, and many not so key, have access to E-mail. So do most individuals who work for your competitor. So do the newspapers and news magazines that are closely following your progress.

Now, what do you think some of the impacts of this technology might be on your organization?

- Scientific management didn't create the assembly line, but the combination of the theory behind that innovation with technological developments in the first part of the twentieth century did. More important, this theory created a whole work culture different from any that had existed before. It not only made possible the creation of automotive giants like Ford and General Motors; it created giant industrial unions like the United Auto Workers. Then refinements of the basic technology made possible the emergence of "lean production," first at Toyota and then at the other automotive manufacturers. In turn, lean production dramatically shifted how workers participate in these automotive industries (and changed the relationship between management and labor significantly). No one at the turn of the century could have predicted the impact the assembly line would have, and no one apparently predicted the impact that "lean production" would have on automobile manufacturers throughout the world.

- The development of "instant" foods of one kind or another and of fast-food restaurants, both quite technology-dependent, was expected to ease the lives of housewives. Instead, it was a significant factor in permitting them to enter the workplace in unheard-of numbers. In turn, this has led in the 1990s to a concern over the plight of latchkey children and with the effect on parenting when both parents work.

The unpredictable impact that technology has on organizations reflects a basic concept in contemporary evolutionary theory: emergent behavior. When subsystems combine, the resultant behavior of the system as a whole is often unpredictable. Who could have predicted the rise of human tool-making from the possession of an opposable thumb? And who can predict the behavior of an organization from its use of a new technology? Increasingly greater unpredictability arises from the impact of new technological subsystems on the organization as a whole. And this brings us to the third aspect of technology, the most interesting and potentially the most powerful aspect.

The Coevolution of Organizations With Their Technology

When an organization adopts a technology that fills a valid business need, it often begins to coevolve with that technology. The development of the assembly line early in the twentieth century created such a situation for automobile companies. As the companies developed, they refined the assembly line to meet their needs, but at the same time the technology of the assembly line forced these same companies to change in certain directions and not in others. And, as you would expect in any true evolutionary situation, Japanese companies evolved in very different ways vis-à-vis their technology than did American companies.

How is coevolving with technology different from simply being affected by it? A story about Compaq Computer provides an example.

Business Week ran a short article in its March 20, 1995, issue on a new forecasting model adopted by Compaq Computer.[2] On the surface, it was about a company adopting a small piece of new technology. Read at a deeper level, though, it provided a dramatic example of the potential for a technology and a company to evolve together.

Trying to improve its competitive position, Compaq created a highly complex forecasting model, designed to predict the major moves of both its competitors and its markets. Presumably, most of its competitors have at least attempted to build the same kind of model. From one point of view, the model constitutes a systematic way of getting environmental inputs. It includes input from customers, from dealers, from suppliers—and almost certainly, though the article doesn't mention it, input about competitors.

Again, on the surface, this seems hardly exceptional. Note, however, that the model systematically presents a wide variety of data (and thus of potential information) about the environment. This enables Compaq to assimilate the information, if it chooses to do so, relatively quickly and efficiently.

Compaq did assimilate the information, with an interesting and important result. The company has prided itself on bringing new technology to market before its competitors did. But the simulation suggested that a new strategy—continuing to sell machines based on the older 486 chips and postponing new lines based on pentiums—would be more profitable. Thus the model identified a strategy that was almost 180 degrees opposed to the historic strategy of the company.

The information in the model prevailed. Compaq stuck with less expensive machines based on the 486 chip for several months longer—and its earnings for the fourth quarter of 1994 rose by 61 percent, presumably as a result of the change in strategy.

What really happened? Compaq evolved in response to the impact of its technology—the forecasting model. At the time the *Business Week* article was written, the company intended to expand the role played by that model. It was embarked on a cyclical process, in which the input from the model pushes the company to change, and as the company changes it forces changes in the model. And unless a major crisis occurs, this coevolution will continue.

Thus a company's internal technology can be a source of coevolution, as changes in the company push evolutionary changes in the technology, which in turn push the company to evolve in a direction it would not otherwise have taken. Compaq Computer and its forecasting model were featured in *Business Week*. Most changes that reflect the coevolution of companies with their technology never will be, but these changes will be just as real:

- Remember Baxter and its terminals everywhere in customer hospitals? Where does the technology lead? It begins to create what amounts to a virtual corporation by seamlessly integrating Baxter's network with the hospitals' information systems. This integration will lead both supplier and customers to evolve in ways that would have been inconceivable without the technology, which in turn will then push the technology in a direction it would not otherwise have gone.

- In her excellent book *In the Age of the Smart Machine,* Shoshana Zuboff describes the impact of the automation of the processes of a pulp mill. After a learning period, workers began to understand the underlying processes more deeply and to react more intelligently to them. Use of the technology began to increase the workers' understanding of the process and their ability to deal with it. This might have led to a significant evolution of the workers' roles and quite possibly to further evolution of the technology. It didn't. The workers believed that their new contributions deserved higher pay. The company didn't, so the workers simply backed off and returned to their previous lower level of contribution.

- Zuboff and others have pointed out a fundamental change that is occurring—probably at an increasing rate—as organizations automate (or, in her terms, infomate). As work comes more and more to depend on understanding and manipulating information, it becomes more abstract. Workers (and managers) react not to physical events but to screens of graphic and textual symbols. This changes both the nature and the demands of the work. Then, as workers become more skilled at handling symbols as a substitute for physical objects, the demands they make on the technology change.

- One final, explosive example: As I write these words, the realization is sinking more deeply into corporate consciousness that computing and communicating power are approaching the point where they are for all practical purposes "free." Not literally free, of course, but the costs of computing and communicating are essentially trivial. Computing power per dollar continues to skyrocket. So does transmission speed. What happens in and to an organization when the cost of computing and the cost of communicating drive its decisions marginally, if at all? We have no idea, but happen it will. And the organization will respond. We can only guess what the result will be in ten or twenty years.

Coevolution Is Everywhere, and It's Unpredictable

We have concentrated on the coevolution between organizations and technology because we still don't appreciate fully the impact this is having on our organizations. Whatever the technology, however, it's part of a much broader context. Every component of an organization participates in the organization's evolution. Every component coevolves with every other component and with the organization as a whole.

This coevolution occurs endlessly, minute by minute, and often out of sight. It may be initiated by an organization-wide conversion from a mainframe computer system to a client-server architecture. It may be initiated by the hiring of a new worker or manager whose unique perspective interacts with others in the organization over time to produce almost imperceptible but real evolution. (Ford Motor probably didn't pay much attention when it hired Alex Trotman in 1955. But his interactions with the company and the individuals in it over the next thirty years resulted in his selection as CEO and his subsequent redirection of the company.) In fact, any organization of any size has a real problem keeping up to date on how it is evolving internally. Everyone in the organization, up to and including the CEO, operates from a simplified stereotype of the organization, and when these stereotypes aren't constantly updated they can lead to unrealistic decisions.

The reverse is also true. When an organization is sensitive

to its internal changes and develops the ability to "listen to it-self," it significantly reduces the amount of internal unpredict-ability and increases the amount of relevant information available to it. Where TQM is implemented successfully, it has this impact; the information flow from the shop floor interacts with management's information flow about broader aspects of company operation, and each enhances the other. And by in-creasing the information flow, the organization increases its abil-ity to evolve effectively both internally and in its relationship to its environment. In short, the more an organization is aware both of its internal states and of the state of its environment, the stronger its competitive position will be.

How does the organization accomplish this? How could your organization accomplish this? Not easily. We've already seen that organizations convert environmental and internal ideas and data into information on the basis of their current state. We've seen the dangers that this creates, as potentially use-ful ideas and data slip through the net because they fail to "fit" the organization's current state—and most novel ideas and most data on unexpected events will fall into this group. But without some selection criteria, some standard for sifting truly useful information from the seemingly endless stream of data available, the organization will be overwhelmed by the data. In the rest of the book I will get very practical about how *not* to be over-whelmed.

Don't Just Anticipate the Unpredictable—Create It

Only one strategy beats that of being able to respond quickly to unexpected events—the ability to create unexpected events that your competitors have to wrestle with.

I have described the payoff from new ideas in a previous book:

> Constant creativity permits the organization to develop
> practices, processes, products, and services that are (1)
> new, (2) relevant to the organization's strategy, and (3)

loaded with value for the organization, its customers, and its stakeholders. When an enterprise continually produces these new practices, processes, products, and services it maintains its competitive position vis-à-vis its competitors—*because they cannot successfully antici-pate what it will do.*[3]

Outside the human realm, biological evolution expresses its endless creativity primarily through the mechanism of random variation and natural selection. At the human level, however, creativity becomes conscious. When an organization can gener-ate and harness the creativity of its members on a continuing basis, it supercharges its ability to evolve in successful ways. Thus any organization that intends to be a successfully evolving organization must be a successfully and constantly creating or-ganization.

The next three chapters contain specific recommendations on how you and your organization can accomplish this most effectively.

8

We've Gotta Get Self-Organized

Very simple organisms are "organized" by the impact of the stimuli in their environment. The more complex organisms become, however, the more their organization becomes self-organization. At the human level, *all* organization is based on self-organization.

Self-Organization Is What There Is

In 1977, Ilya Prigogine, a Belgian scientist, won the Nobel Prize for his work with what he called "dissipative systems"—which have subsequently been dubbed "self-organizing systems." His discoveries set off a wave of interest in self-organizing systems among physicists, chemists, biologists, and organizational theorists. Unfortunately, the closer the scientific theory has gotten to organizational theory the fuzzier and more misleading it has become. When human beings are concerned, "self-organization" means something very different from what it does at the physical or biological level.

The heart of Prigogine's discoveries was simple: Local order can be created in violation of the second law of thermodynamics. The second law of thermodynamics holds that the universe is dying a "heat death." Whenever changes occur that affect energy, heat is dissipated and the system moves from order to disorder.

Prigogine found that at a local, limited level, a system could create negative entropy by drawing energy from its environment and using it to increase its own internal organization. This discovery, that order could arise spontaneously from disorder, has become one of the underpinnings of the contemporary science of chaos and complexity theory. Biologists are applying it to evolutionary theory, and management theorists are applying it to organizational theory.

Unfortunately, there is a catch. We do not need to import a theory from physics, chemistry, or biology to start finding out how human beings can self-organize themselves and their organizations. The fundamental fact is this:

All human organization is self-organization. Period.

All functioning human beings organize themselves. If a panhandler hits you for a handout on the street, the odds are two out of three that he is either a drug addict or mentally ill. But the odds are three out of three that he has organized his behavior to be able to ask for the handout. He was undoubtedly heavily influenced by his parents, his home environment, his school environment, his adult experiences, life on the street, and other factors even he may not recognize. But only he could take all these influences and organize them, poorly or well, into a functioning human being.[1]

Organizational theory since Taylor and scientific management has hidden this basic fact from us. So has our emphasis on the assembly line and other routinized production processes. So has our single-minded devotion to organizational charts—as though they somehow captured reality in tight little boxes. We have swallowed the idea that people have to be organized and that once we "organize" them they operate that way until we "reorganize" them.

The irony is this: We have known for at least three decades that this paints a distorted and perhaps just plain wrong picture of how organizations really function. The picture first began to come into focus when organizational psychologists and sociologists discovered the "informal" organization that seemed to coexist with the "formal" organization. They discovered that individuals created and used relationships that bore no necessary resemblance whatsoever to the "reality" the little boxes represented.

Earlier I described some of the ways in which the real internal structures of organizations operate. I don't need to add to that description here, except for one very telling point. Organization charts, whatever else they do, are supposed to draw lines of authority. Combined with position descriptions, these should give an outside observer a clear idea of the kind and degree of authority and control exerted and of the freedom allowed to subordinate positions. Except that they don't. Studies have found that the way authority relationships actually work in an organization generally correlates so poorly with the formal description of them as to make the formal description practically useless.

Nor should this surprise us. I have repeatedly stressed that all change is individual. If countries appear to change, it's because thousands or millions of individuals in them changed. If organizations appear to change, it's because hundreds or thousands of individuals in them changed. Self-organization is a basic form of change, so all self-organization is the self-organization of the individual. (Highly cohesive teams are based on and are a partial extension of individual self-organization; we will deal with them in a later section.)

At their heart, magnificent organizational edifices such as General Electric, Ford, or 3M are created and maintained by the self-organization of the individuals who compose them—no matter how carefully their organizational charts disguise this fact.

Self-Organization: Getting From Here to Where?

That self-organization is basic can't be denied. But how effective this self-organization is presents an entirely different problem. The panhandler on the street may be self-organized, but only at a very basic level. Unfortunately, all too many individuals entering the work force seem to organize themselves at an only slightly higher level. In 1990, the National Center on Education and the Economy published *America's Choice: high skills or low wages!* The interviews with employers on which the book was based indicated that companies were satisfied with the range of technical skills (or lack of skills) that current high-school graduates possess. However, these same employers were largely dissatisfied with these same graduates' ability to effectively organize their own behavior.[2]

Put these words into the context of today's competitive world. Virtually every change in the organization of people for the past thirty years has required more effective self-organization and self-management from them. At least in theory, assembly-line workers in the Michigan of the 1950s and 1960s had to do very little organizing of themselves. They needed to show up, perform their engineered jobs over and over in the same way, and collect their paychecks. Then look at the organization of the Saturn plant in the 1990s; there workers perform as part of close-knit teams and participate in virtually every level of decision making in the plant. The Saturn organization represents a true quantum jump in the self-organizational and self-management skills required.

So does every use of self-managing teams within organizations. Most books on teams stress the need for group-oriented skills: conflict resolution, teamwork, negotiation, and so on. They're needed, but they're second-level skills. No team can adopt and use these skills unless its members are first of all effective at organizing themselves. For example, how can a team effectively resolve conflict unless its members can constructively manage the conflict within themselves? A worker who responds to all criticism as an attack on his self-esteem (a basic symptom of poor self-organization) won't contribute much to the team's attempts to resolve its internal conflicts.

Individual Self-Organization

If self-organization counts for more and more in contemporary organizations, what must individuals—and thus organizations—do to become self-organized? Every field that currently deals with organizations, from chaos theory through behavior-ism to cybernetics, has its own recipe for self-organization. If we were to throw them all into a bag and shake them up well, what came out might look a lot like the following seven requirements for individual self-organization.

1. *The individual has to have relatively clear and specific goals.* Human self-organization begins by formulating goals, goals that are clear enough to allow an individual knowingly to pursue them. The goals may change, and one characteristic of increas-ingly more effective self-organization is that they do change. But there must be goals. Some of these may be very long-term goals, but they are supported by much shorter-term and immediate goals, so that the individual is constantly pursuing clearly achievable goals.

2. *The goals are sufficiently important that the individual will spend the time and effort required to accomplish them.* Everyone has desires, and most of us could come up with a splendid list of things we'd like to accomplish. But, as they say, a desire and 50 cents won't get you a cup of coffee in most places today. What counts is not desires but goals—goals supported by the clear *intent* to accomplish them. Put even more practically, what counts are goals that the individual believes are worth the effort that it will take to achieve them. For individuals to self-organize their lives, they must have a strong sense of what matters enough to them for them to devote the necessary time and en-ergy to get it. Typically, we all learn through trial and error what really matters this much to us, and the learning itself is an intrin-sic part of self-organizing.

3. *The individual has it within his or her power to achieve the goals.* No aspect of self-organization is more ambiguous than this. On the one hand, it makes little sense to pursue goals be-yond one's power to achieve. Most of us would waste significant amounts of our lives if we set out to become opera singers, stock car racers, or medical researchers. But not all of us—and it would be difficult to tell in the beginning who would succeed and who wouldn't. Perhaps the most important words here are those of Charlie Pride, the country and western singer. Someone

once commented to Charlie that he sure had been lucky. "I certainly have," Charlie replied. "But, you know, it's a funny thing—the harder I work the luckier I get."

4. *The individual has or develops the competence required to accomplish the goals.* Every step of self-organizing requires competence. The process itself requires competence at setting goals and selecting the steps required to achieve them. Then the individual must learn and use the skills required to accomplish the goals themselves. Opera singers, stock car racers, and medical researchers must develop the skills their occupations require. These and most other occupations identify the competence required for success. If your goal is a happy marriage, the competencies aren't quite as clear. And they may be murkier still if your goal is to find lasting happiness. But every goal, from minute to immense, requires competence to achieve.

5. *The individual can get information from the environment relevant to the goals and her progress toward them.* The ability to achieve goals depends utterly on feedback—information about the environment and the effects of one's actions on that environment. Visualize a worker who wants to get ahead in her job. First, she needs to know what kinds of behaviors and accomplishments are valued by the organization. Then, if she can get the answer to that question, she needs to know how others see her performance. The information she gets must also have one other characteristic: She must get it in time to use it to change her actions. Suppose she finds out after a peer has been promoted that innovation is prized more than cost-consciousness. That doesn't help a lot, does it? Information in general and feedback in particular are time-bound; their usefulness depends on *when* the individual gets them.

6. *The individual can assimilate this feedback so that he can use it to change his actions to become more successful at achieving the goal.* We often get so caught up in mechanical models of information and feedback that we forget that nothing in the process is automatic. To be used, information must be processed, and that means it must be understood, assimilated, and used by the individual to shape his future actions. This is where the learning occurs, and if this part of the process fails the process as a whole

fails with it. When someone executes this step effectively, we typically say that he has good judgment. And, typically, each of us learns to exercise good judgment by experiencing multiple instances in which we exercised not-quite-so-good judgment.

7. *The individual is opportunistic and able to take advantage of random, unexpected events.* Earlier chapters should have demonstrated how bound organizations are to their mental models of what matters in the world, and how resistant they are to ideas and data that don't fit these models. Individuals operate in the same way. (Of course they do, because their individual decisions are what make up organizational decisions.) The ability to identify and use relevant unexpected data—to profit from serendipity—separates individuals who get stuck at one level of self-organization from those who move to continually higher and higher levels.

Each individual must possess all these characteristics to at least some degree in order to self-organize his life. Far more important for the purposes of this book, however, any team or other organizational unit that intends to be self-organizing must also possess them, as well as several other necessary characteristics.

Self-Organizing Teams

Peter Senge regards teams as the fundamental units of the learning organization. Certainly they can be such. But no magic ensures that a team will be a self-organizing, self-directing, complex adaptive (learning) system. Teams require individual members who have learned how to organize their own behavior. Then the team itself must meet the same seven requirements at the team level to become self organizing:

1. *The team must have a clear mission supported by clear goals.* Some organizations, particularly those that have encouraged and supported worker-level empowerment for years, can operate with teams whose missions are somewhat fuzzy. Most organizations can't. Much more so than with individuals, team

missions and the goals supporting these missions must be clear to all members of the team. When work is performed by a team instead of an individual, the requirements for communication and coordination rise sharply. The team's mission should be the basis for this communication, not something that has to be discussed and reformulated time and time again.

2. *The goals must be sufficiently important that the team and its members will commit themselves to accomplishing them.* Members of successful teams work hard to achieve that success. But they work hard only when they believe that the team's mission and goals are worth the effort. Teams with trivial assignments produce trivial results.

3. *The team must have it within its power to achieve the goals.* In somewhat fancier language, a team must control its critical success factors. A team pumped up to improve its processes will deflate quickly when confronted by an intractable data system. So will a team that comes up with a new product only to find that it crashes and burns because of the "not invented here" mentality of a key department. One of Lee Iacocca's last and greatest achievements at Chrysler was the creation of highly empowered teams that were able to design a string of automotive successes—because they needed only a bare minimum of approvals from Iacocca or anyone else.

4. *The team must have or develop the competence required to accomplish its goals.* Individuals need high competence to organize themselves and produce successful results, and so do teams. But members of teams need two very different kinds of competence. They need to be highly competent at what they contribute as individuals, and they need to be just as competent at making this contribution as part of a team. In short, for individuals to operate successfully as members of teams rather than as individual workers, they must increase their overall competence significantly.

5. *The team must be able to get feedback—information from the environment relevant to its goals and its progress toward them.* The more quickly a team can get information on its current success in meeting its goals, the more quickly it can improve its performance. What does *quickly* mean? It means getting feedback in time

to improve *current* performance—not getting it as a post facto evaluation of past performance. Take this to the bank: The more prompt, specific, and useful the feedback is, the better the performance will be.

6. *The team must be able to assimilate this information and use it to change its actions to become more successful at achieving the goal.* Since the early 1980s, the focus on quality programs and self-directing work teams in manufacturing environments has emphasized feedback on relatively routine and easily understood processes. As teams move outward from the shop floor, however, feedback ceases to be so cut and dried. When 3M test-marketed Post-It Notes, the feedback from the test was anything but simple and easy to interpret. Teams must increasingly possess competence at both analysis and synthesis to respond effectively to their environments.

7. *The team must be opportunistic and able to take advantage of random, unexpected events.* Individuals, teams, and organizations that want to evolve successfully must be open to events and ideas they cannot predict. They must somehow combine their focus on the environment, which gives them the information and feedback they know they need, with a way of being open to the unexpected. One of the great strengths of the Zen-influenced art of Japan has been its ability to use a solid, careful technique that was at the same time open to, and that incorporated, random occurrences—such as the dripping of an overly full brush into a bowl. Organizations must create their own version of this strength to survive.

Unfortunately, a team can possess every one of these seven characteristics of self-organization and still fail, perhaps miserably so, if it lacks one final characteristic:

8. *An effective team must be a group of individuals who believe they need each other to act successfully.* In my book *Teampower* I used this notion (coined by Arie de Geus) as the fundamental definition of a team. The intervening years have convinced me that this definition is, if anything, even more critical than I thought it to be at the time. Teams are really teams only when their members believe that they each need each other for the team to succeed. A few "extra" people, added to a team because

there was no other good place to put them, will begin to handicap the team in one of two ways. They will have no real function, leading other members of the team to see them as deadwood who interfere with the work of the team; or they will make valiant attempts to find jobs to do that don't really need to be done, again interfering with the team's performance.

How can even one unnecessary member have this impact? To succeed, a team must be cohesive; it must think of itself as a single operating entity, not as a collection of individual workers. (The well-known formula for team building, Forming, Storming, Norming, Performing, is at heart a recipe for developing cohesion.) Cohesion is strengthened to the extent that team members perceive a real need for each other. It is weakened to the extent that they do not. Moral? When you create a team, err on the side of putting too few members on it, not too many.

The Role of "Flow" in Self-Organization

For more than two decades, Mihaly Csikszentmihalyi, professor of psychology at the University of Chicago, has been conducting research to identify what makes people happy, both on the job and off. Perhaps surprisingly, perhaps not, he has come up with some solid results. People are at their happiest when they are in what Dr. Csikszentmihalyi calls a "flow" state. What characterizes individuals in this state?

1. They are working to accomplish clear goals.
2. They get immediate feedback about their progress toward these goals.
3. They must use significant skills to achieve their goals.
4. They are in control of the work and have it in their power to accomplish it.
5. They can concentrate on the goals without being distracted.
6. They become deeply involved in the work.
7. They focus on the work and lose concern for themselves.
8. They experience an altered sense of time.

9. They consistently produce at high levels of accomplishment.

The characteristics fall into three groups. The first five characterize the work and the worker's relationship to it. Compare the characteristics with the seven requirements for self-organization and you will see how similar they are. Characteristics six through eight describe the individual's reactions to work that place him in a flow state. Just as easily, one can rephrase this and say that these are the reactions of an individual operating at a high level of self-organization. The final characteristic says this: If Dr. Csikszentmihalyi is right, when an individual is in a flow state, he or she achieves the highest level of performance possible at that point in time.

Make no mistake about it, this is heady stuff. While Dr. Csikszentmihalyi's ideas will figure prominently in the remainder of this book, I recommend in the strongest possible terms that you read at least his book *Flow: The Psychology of Optimal Experience* and think deeply about its implications for self-organization and your organization.

Self-Organization: The Lessons

At the turn from the twentieth to the twenty-first century, companies that can consistently foster internal self-organization will survive. No—they will *thrive*. Companies that can't further self-organization may survive, and a few of them may even thrive, but their path will be harder and riskier. And no company can have both the supposed safety and predictability of a traditional top-down organization and the initiative and responsiveness of a continually self-organizing, self-reorganizing internal structure.

Suppose you want to consider and perhaps adopt a highly self-organizing internal structure based on teams—either continuing teams or project teams. What critical success factors should you consider? Here are six of them:

1. Be Realistic About What Self-Organizing Teams Require

If you attempt to change your organization so that it's composed of self-organizing teams, expect that one of three results will occur. You will succeed, in which case you will change the overall organization beyond belief. Or you will fail, and then spend countless hours and resources (including management time and money) trying to struggle back to where you were. Or, perhaps the worst alternative of all, the change will run out of steam, lose momentum, and die in place without ever being formally buried. Think the choice through, because each of the options (including success) will be disruptive as hell. Then, if you want to try it, accept these basic truths:

- In the short run, even in the most effective program, *the organization will endure not only confusion but chaos.* Don't think that the word *chaos* is an exaggeration; if you're serious about moving to self-organization, chaos will happen. Expect it, accept it, and create space for it. And when it happens, and it's far worse than you imagined, just keep going. You can get through it to the other side and discover a completely different kind of order.

- In the short run, the longer run, and perhaps even the longest run, *it will feel as if you're losing control.* In the conventional management sense, you will be. Self-organizing teams, or other similar units, are also self-managing. They literally cannot be managed by higher levels in any useful sense. They can be led, and led very effectively—and you will find turning from traditional management to empowered leadership quite challenging enough to your own ability to learn and change. When you make the turn, you will also find that leading an empowered organization is far more fun than trying to manage a traditional one.

- Start now to *improve communication within the organization, and improve it substantially.* When you begin to implement self-organization, things will, at best, go only partly as planned. Without truly effective and open communications, the naysayers will fill the grapevine with accounts of how the organization was dumb to try it in the first place and how it's failing now. Supporters may feel isolated and vulnerable, wondering if they should fold their hands and join the naysayers. But if the organization abandons its usual puffery and replaces it with basic honesty, if it identifies the problems and how they're being corrected, and if it accurately presents the successes, it will maintain its supporters and quite possibly begin to get grudging support from early opponents. And, though you shouldn't count on this, the organization may face the happy problem that more units want to become self-organizing than it can deal with. Don't count on it, but don't count it out, either.

- Remember, *if you succeed, the overall organization will change beyond belief.* You can't produce this change on a schedule; it will happen in its own time and of its own accord. Just accept that it will, in fact, happen, and prepare yourself and the organization accordingly. Then go about making the change.

- Finally, remember what I've said about transformational change: At least two times out of three, it fails. You can end up in the 33 percent group only by taking two steps: (1) Do the analysis and planning required to ensure that self-organization is really a viable option for your organization; (2) commit yourself and your management team to making self-organization succeed—which means that it will probably be your primary task for the next few years. Can't make the commitment? If not, don't start the process.

2. Focus the Implementation Carefully

If your organization is like most, it's made up of (1) individuals and managers who should become self-organizing; (2) individuals and managers who want to be self-organizing (because it's fashionable and/or a quick way to get noticed), but either can't handle it now or are in units that shouldn't be self-organizing; (3) individuals and managers who want to avoid whatever "self-organization" is like the plague; and (4) the largest group consisting individuals and managers who want to crouch back in the weeds and find out what's going to happen before they commit themselves. If you want self-organization to succeed, you must focus intently and intelligently on where to implement it.

- Where do you begin? *Find an area where managers and workers are willing to try it and where it makes sense to try it.* (If there's a conflict between willingness and appropriateness, lean toward willingness.) Because implementation is hard work, you want individuals who have the initial motivation to do that hard work. Start with a few teams. They can be continuing teams; perhaps the time has come to set up a self-organizing team that includes both sales and the individuals required to fulfill the sales. Perhaps they should be project teams to develop new products or services.

- *Work out careful, clear milestones that are tied to specific results if possible.* Don't trust to some gods of self-organization to accomplish this for you. Set reasonable, meaningful milestones—preferably in concert with the team(s) involved—that will keep you informed of what's happening. If you need others along when you meet with the team(s) at these points, fine, but make it clear that the meeting is between *you* and the team(s). Delegate this responsibility to a staff office somewhere and you may as well forget it and save much time and effort.

- *Provide a way for the team to get feedback.*

- *Provide the necessary support, then get out of their way.* See that the team(s) get the necessary training. Provide expert facilitators. Provide direct access to you if conditions require it. Then let them go about self-organizing. If Lee Iacocca could set up self-organizing project teams to design cars and then get out of their way, you certainly can.

- *Use their success to recruit others.* Self-organizing teams need a certain amount of anonymity, at first, to get themselves organized and operating. Then, when they begin to produce results, publicize these results. Ensure that the entire organization knows of their successes (but first make sure that they truly are successes). You don't want isolated successes; you want the rest of the organization beating on your door to become self-organizing. No matter how many sign up, you still want to focus on the high-probability managers and units. Don't rule out the initial naysayers, though; some of them may show up, hat in hand, to join the parade. Let them, that's a trophy catch!

3. Develop a Clear Team Mission

Teams succeed when the members need each other to accomplish a fully intelligible mission. Unless the overall organization is exceptionally effective at self-organization, teams with cloudy or ill-defined missions will flounder and quite possibly end up causing more problems than they solve. Most books on team organization begin with the so-called team-building phase. That puts the cart before the horse. First, define the mission for the team. You don't need to make the mission airtight at this point, but make it clear. Keep these points in mind:

- *Help guarantee the success of the team by focusing the mission on a customer or group of customers and/or on a specific process or product.* The best possible mission combines a clearly defined product or service and a clearly defined customer or customer group.
- This can get a bit tricky, but *let the team contribute to define the mission as much as possible.* Initially, the organization will probably do best by providing the mission statement and focusing the team on it. As the team starts to jell, however, it will begin to understand the ramifications and limitations of the mission better than those who initially formulated it. From that point on, the team should be an active participant in modifying the mission. This is not a set process or a one-way one. It depends on the mission, the way the organization is changing, the capabilities and interests of the team—a host of factors.
- Once the team becomes an effective one, *make refining and updating the mission a regular milestone.* Once a month? Once a quarter? Once a year? It depends completely on the team, your organization, and the rate of change. If you err, err on the side of asking the question whether and how it needs to change too frequently, not too rarely. The mission will focus the team; part of the organization's responsibility is ensuring that the team fo-

cuses on what will contribute the greatest value to the organization. If you do not focus the mission and update it whenever necessary, you prevent the team from making its maximum contribution—and quite possibly doom it to being less effective than the traditional work group it replaced.

4. Provide Effective Feedback Systems

A team can be no more effective than the quality of the feedback it gets. Period.

First, let's remember exactly what feedback is. It is *not* monthly, quarterly, or annual "feedback" from a manager as to how an individual, team, or organization did in some previous time period. It is *not* general information about performance results, no matter where it comes from. *Feedback is specific, direct, prompt information about progress toward goals received by an individual, team, or organization in time to improve current performance.* If it fails to meet this definition, whatever you call feedback is probably wasting more time, effort, and money to provide than its meager benefits warrant. How do you fix it?

• Technology may be useful, but don't begin there. *Focus on getting specific, direct, prompt information about the results they're achieving to the teams that need it* (and to the individuals on the teams, if necessary). If a manager or staff office needs the same information, give it to them, but give it to them in addition to giving it to the team. Individuals and teams can make far better use of feedback that comes directly to them than of feedback that's filtered through someone else.

Why is this true? When a supervisor gets the information and passes it on, he cannot help but color it by his own concerns. For instance, has he been under pressure to reduce errors? If so, the information will be filtered through this concern. You cannot avoid it; feedback passed through an intermediary will ultimately be information on how to please that intermediary. Unless you intend that to be the basic goal of the team—and if it is, why are you talking about *self*-organization?—you need for the team to get feedback directly.

▪ *Make it clear that the team is to use the feedback to improve performance.* Managers and/or staff offices can play a truly useful role here by making sure that the team understands the feedback and then showing it how to use it most effectively. With luck, this won't take long, and team members can then start using it on their own. From that point on, no one else should intervene unless the team fails to use the feedback effectively.

▪ Performers will in fact respond to the clearest and most useful feedback they get, so *make sure that the feedback received by the team concerns the most important aspects of its goals.* Here's an example. Suppose you tell the team that you want high quality from it, but most of the praise or blame it gets concerns the speed with which it produces. Which do you believe it will concentrate on—quality or speed?

▪ Finally, *realize that you will never get a fully adequate, comprehensive feedback system in place.* Start with the best you can get, then improve on it. No, start with the best you can get and then let the team tell you how to improve on it. Then do so. The interaction between goals as the team understands them and the feedback they get and can use will completely drive the team's performance. If you want truly effective performance, see that the goals are clear and that the feedback is specific, direct, and prompt. Then get out of the way unless and until the team asks for your help. Go do strategy!

5. Support the Team With Appropriate Technology and Systems

Don't think for a moment that technology doesn't matter. It does, it matters very much. And what matters most of all is this: *The technology must directly support self-organization by the team*—as must all your organizational systems.

Stop and think for a moment. Weren't your technology and systems developed to support a traditional, top-down, hierarchical organization? Don't they support performance driven from higher levels? Don't they provide information primarily to higher-level managers and staff offices rather than to the performers? Don't they reward conformance to higher-level directives and minimal risk taking? Many teams can overcome this kind of inertia in the initial rush of developing a mission, organizing themselves, and taking off. But not forever. Unless changes are made in the old, hierarchical reality, it begins to smother the team's initiative. Your job is to make sure this never happens by making the changes necessary to support the teams.

- Don't be surprised if *nothing* in your existing computer systems seems useful for supporting self-organizing teams. In fact, expect that initially your current technology will contribute far more to the problem than it does to the solution.

- So will your existing systems and procedures. *Look at your reward system*—the full system, not just the official compensation system. What gets people promoted? What keeps them from getting fired, or from being shunted into dead-end jobs? What *really* wins them their "merit" raises? Probably not initiative, the willingness to argue for what they believe in, or the ability to challenge established ways of doing things. And what does the human resources system emphasize—safety (no EEO complaints), equity (no harsh distinctions on the basis of performance), perhaps even procedural completeness (at the expense of speed in filling orders)?

- If this is the case, *don't try to change everything at once!* In fact, don't try to change much by yourself. Get the teams up and going. Then go to them and ask them where the problems are. Attack those problems, picking the easy and quick ones first.

- Even where teams are most successful, compensation poses a major problem. There is no simple solution. Expect problems, and keep working on them. No one yet has found *the* answer, and many organizations have yet to find even acceptable answers.

6. Expect Very Different Kinds of Problems

If you've been a manager for long, you know that changes can solve problems, but that whether they solve them or not they are sure to cause new problems. The results of building an organization around self-organization will be no different. Done right, self-organization will make your company much more flexible and responsive than it has been, and perhaps increase both quality and productivity in the process. As it does, these are some of the issues self-organization will raise:

• How can the organization maintain effective integration and coordination when its components are self-organizing and self-managing? We've already looked at the constant internal evolution (or lack of it) caused by competition for resources, power, and status among different functions within the organization. The internal competition will change significantly as self-organization becomes a reality, but it will not go away.

• Self-organization requires access to and effective use of an information flow on an order of magnitude greater than that found in traditional organizations. How does the organization reduce the information to manageable proportions without filtering out the ideas and data that don't fit its preconceptions? How does it ensure that the individuals and units that need it get it?

• What will the career paths be? In a traditional organization, individuals move up clearly defined functional stovepipes through layer after layer of management. Everyone can keep score and separate the fast-trackers from those who are being shunted aside. But the more that an organization is self-organizing and self-managing, the fewer the stovepipes and the fewer the layers there are to provide upward progress. We don't yet know what meaning a "career path" will have in an organization like this; all we know is that it will be very different from career paths in the past.

Is This Still Evolution?

Are we still dealing with organizational evolution? Yes. But we have expanded our scope. Human beings are self-organizing in a way that no other creatures we know of are. Human self-organization is an extension of biological evolution—but also a quantum jump from what has occurred before. Our ability to organize our individual and group behavior has enabled us to build societies across the face of the globe and to embody past learning in culture so that no generation has to begin anew.

One of the most surprising and most successful forms of self-organization is the system we call free enterprise. Let's examine it—not as a method of national economic organization but as a means of *internal* organization based on self-organization.

9

Taking Adam Smith Seriously: Creating a Free Market Within Your Organization

Evolution, in nature and in organizations, is completely dependent on the variety of options that can be generated and the effectiveness of those that are implemented. Nature evolves by creating variety through random variation and implementation through natural selection. An organization can evolve most successfully not by centralized command and control of resources but by an internal free market—because it excels at both creating variations and implementing the best ones.

When we look at organizations from an evolutionary perspective, we find that change is constant and there are multiple paths to the future; that the available paths both promise a payoff and cut the organization off from other paths; that the change that actually occurs can never be adequately forecast or controlled, because it is created, moment by moment, from the interaction (coevolution) of all the players involved; and, as a result, the future remains unpredictable, both in theory and in fact.

In this kind of world, the most successful companies must generate a wide variety of alternatives to select from, and then choose the best alternatives to implement. Yes, product development groups can perform this function. Yes, brainstorming can enable a group of workers, managers, or whoever to come up with a variety of ideas. But this is the key fact:

> *There is no way of developing and selecting from a variety of alternatives that is as effective as a market economy.*

Does this surprise you? Probably, because Western organizational theory decided well over a century ago that free enterprise, desirable as it was on a national level, had no place within modern industrial organizations. Well, I think this was the wrong decision. In this chapter, I will do my best to show you why and how to free yourself from this mistake.

The Truth Behind Free Enterprise

In our day and age, the core ideas of democracy are obscured by concerns about political parties, political action groups, equitable distribution of voting power, and all the mechanics of a political system. From the beginning in ancient Athens, however, there has been a core, and this core forms the basis of any democratic system. What is that core?

- Ordinary individuals are competent to make the decisions by which they will live.
- The best environment in which to make these decisions is one in which ideas compete with one another for attention and action.
- The democratic process succeeds when it generates a variety of ideas, develops and evaluates the ideas, and then selects the most successful ideas for testing.

It takes little thought to realize that this is the basic free market process applied to ideas. In a functioning democracy, people choose the ideas by which they will live from a variety of competing ideas. However, they do so not by blindly selecting from whatever ideas happen to be easily available but by actively searching for and generating ideas and then developing and evaluating them to find the best. So, if we focus on the free-market aspect of democracy we can leave the rest of the baggage to the political process and work with the part that has the highest payoff for the organization—intelligent selection from a wide variety of options.

We view a free market in goods and services as an "economic" system and a free market in ideas as a "political" system. This creates an artificial distinction. Neither reaches its maximum effectiveness without the other. Both are highly effective processes for generating alternatives, then developing and evaluating them so that the best can be tested and implemented.

These free markets not only accept but assume self-organization throughout society. In fact, a free market of any kind has no meaning apart from self-organization. No other system usable in a modern industrial/information society places this reliance on self-organization. So, if self-organization truly forms the key to successful adaptation and competitive success, this alone should lead us to look very, very carefully at the competitive potential of a free market in goods, services, and ideas as an effective organizing principle *within* an organization.

How does a market economy differ from centralized control? It permits individuals and groups to self-organize and produce a variety of products, services, and ideas from which consumers select those that provide the best value. How does it accomplish this? By enabling these individuals and groups (1) to generate alternatives; (2) to develop and evaluate the alternatives; and (3) to select the best alternatives for testing and implementation. In short, goods, services, and ideas must compete with one another for attention and resources, and the success of this system depends utterly on the extent to which it enables individual and group choices based on a free information flow.

If a free market is so effective, it provides the key to a new and far more powerful way of organizing and operating in a highly competitive environment—and we need to explore that way.

Free Enterprise in a Government Organization?

Some information about my organization illustrates the real power of an internal free market. First, you should know that I am a federal civil servant, and have been so for over thirty years. I worked my way up from trainee through a variety of jobs to management—just the way I would have in a traditional organization. I moved into my present job, as manager of an organization that provides a variety of services primarily to a federal agency about the size of Delta Airlines, in 1987.

You might expect that my management team and I would have followed the stereotypical bureaucratic path from that point on. Expand the organization and its budget during the good times, fight to protect it during the down times. Promote policies in the larger organization to force other parts of the organization to deal with us and emphasize the sanctity of our function. Build and protect an empire. Take the safe path. Provide satisfactory or slightly better performance in return for job and organizational security. *We did none—absolutely none—of that.*

It took us several years, but, with the support of a few key executives, we convinced the agency that it would be best served if it let us become an entrepreneurial organization. For the past several years, we have faced actual or potential competition on every project we have worked on. And we have honestly competed, because we make it clear to our customers that not only are they free to go to an outside source but we will in fact help them. (Yes, we really have done just that.) Our customers, mostly inside the agency, provide us with every cent we get; we receive zero dollars from the agency's central budgeting process.

How do we manage this? By being from 20 percent to 50 percent less expensive for work of at least the same quality than our competitors are. Remember, this is a federal organization, subject to every one of the rigid limitations that all federal organizations are subject to. And we are competing against private firms. But the fact remains that we produce high-quality, usually higher-quality, work at a lower cost. And this saves you and me, the taxpayers, real money.

Why? Because we operate as far as possible as a private enterprise; that is, we believe and act on the premise that we exist to provide unique value to our customers. We commit ourselves to their success first, then to our own. We've had our ups and downs; in a rapidly downsizing agency, the downs are hard to avoid. But we have not only survived but thrived. We have kept our customers. We have been able to offer reasonable job security to our staff. In short, we are competing successfully as a generally free enterprise in the heart of a large government bureaucracy. And we are, as Maxwell Smart used to say, enjoying every minute of it.

The competition extends to ideas. The group is led by a management team composed of myself and four other key managers. I direct the organization, but when the team sits down as a team my voice counts for no more than that of any other team member. We attempt to make decisions by consensus, and only when the disagreement appears unbridgeable—a rarity—will I cast the deciding vote. Our goal is to come up with a variety of ideas, then let the ideas rather than the individuals compete for ultimate success.

The agency has a suggestion program, but virtually no one in our group ever submits suggestions. Instead, everyone understands that they are expected to contribute ideas, and their team leaders and managers are expected to listen to them—carefully. More than that, we expect these team leaders and managers to help individuals develop their ideas.

As I write this, we have a significant problem in the relationship between two key divisions. A team made up of members of both divisions is working on the problem, with the clear understanding that the management team has placed no prior restrictions on the solutions it may develop. The team must be willing to negotiate its solutions with the management team, but that's far different from needing the management team's permission to develop one solution or another.

I haven't written this section to toot my group's merits—though I'm willing to do so at the drop of a hat. I wrote it to give you a glimpse of how powerful an internal free market can be, even in the heart of a giant bureaucracy.

Not everything is rosy, of course. We still work under personnel and procurement systems that value equality more highly than excellence. We cannot carry a profit from one year to another. More important, we work in a total system that is currently focused on reducing head count. We have demonstrated that we can not only compete but perform most work for less than our private competitors. But we are federal employees and part of the head count—so we show on the books as a *cost* to the government, not as an asset.

Why Organizations Resist Internal Markets

We know that a free market in goods, services, and ideas—warts, boils, ingrown toenails, and all—is the best way to organize modern economic life in general. The Soviet empire became extinct for many reasons, not least because it was unable to generate the new products, services, and ideas it needed to compete against the world's market-driven democracies. At present, only Singapore among the major countries of the world is managing to combine a more or less free market with a highly authoritarian government. Whether it can continue this for another generation remains up for grabs. China is trying to follow the same path; its outcome is even more problematic.

We also have anecdotal evidence from my own organization and from a few others (mostly described in Gifford and Elizabeth Pinchot's book *The End of Bureaucracy and the Rise of the Intelligent Corporation*) that internal free enterprise can be very productive. If this is so, why have so few organizations even experimented with it? Why does this approach, so central to so much of our economic thought on a macro level, remain so foreign to American management thought and practice at the company level? I would suggest four basic reasons:

1. The belief that an internal free market would be more chaotic and inefficient than the command-and-control organization of resource providers.
2. The fact that when a variety of goods, services, and ideas is available it is difficult to get, develop, evaluate, and test those that offer the most promise.

3. The fact that given a traditional means of organization and operation, it costs far more to try out a new product, service, or idea than to reproduce or slightly modify an existing one.
4. And, perhaps most important, the fact that when corporate managers experience or even consider internal free enterprise, they feel very much as if they're giving up control.

Because these are all powerful factors, and all quite different from one another, each one deserves a closer look.

1. *An internal free market would be more chaotic and inefficient than the command-and-control organization of resource providers.* In theory, an organization will get the goods, services, and ideas it needs from internal providers by setting up appropriate units to provide them and then managing these units in the same way it manages production and sales. Want new ideas? Set up an R&D department and/or a product development department. Want office supplies and equipment? Set up a department to analyze the organization's needs and procure what's needed at the best price.

We know that this doesn't work on a national level, as the shambles that was the Soviet economy so eloquently testifies. (A cynic might add that the condition of GM and IBM in the late 1980s wasn't radically different.) Then why do we expect it to work within an organization? *Because we have never made a serious attempt to test this approach against an internal free market.*

When American industry began to operate on a large scale in the nineteenth century, what examples were available to it on how to run a large organization? The Roman Catholic Church. The world's armies. The first large enterprises—American railroads. And such historical examples as the Roman Empire, to the extent that managers were interested in them. Then Frederick W. Taylor developed "scientific management," which explicitly required workers to carry out very detailed instructions without thought or deviation. These influences added up to what we would today call the command-and-control model of management. The top echelon makes all the basic decisions (command), then establishes a hierarchy of managers beneath themselves to ensure that the decisions are carried out as intended (control). By the 1960s, the approach was enshrined in the standard textbook planning-organizing-directing-controlling (PODC) model.

This model explicitly ruled out any form of internal market. It especially rejected any form of a market economy in ideas. New ideas were tolerated only in those departments specifically created to spawn them. What appeared so logical and straightforward in the PODC model, however, seemed suddenly second-rate when its embodiment in the American automotive industry had to compete with a Japanese management structure that not only accepted but solicited ideas from throughout the organization.

We still haven't developed an organizational theory that would lead us to try internal free enterprise on any systematic basis. Until that happens, the idea that such a system would be less efficient and/or difficult to control remains just that—an untested idea.

2. *It is difficult to select from a large variety of goods, services, and ideas.* This fact undoubtedly constitutes part of the reason organizations resist having an open market internally, particularly an open market in ideas. Some forty years ago, a psychologist came up with the famous "seven, plus or minus two" limitation on the number of alternatives that an individual or group can genuinely consider when making a decision. The limitation has held up remarkably well over time. While decision makers cry constantly for more information, the information they crave is that which will make their choices simpler, not more extensive. In most organizations, having "decision briefing" in which seventeen alternatives are presented and evaluated without a clear indication of the top two or three virtually guarantees a quick slide onto the slow track.

Not all the free enterprise in the world will gain an organization much if it insists on subjecting everything to this variation-limiting orthodoxy.

Biological evolution uses a very simple process to test variations: It generates an overwhelming number of mutations and waits to see which ones will succeed. This represents the diametric opposite of the typical organizational procedure; the only biological test is final success or failure. Unfortunately, while individuals and organizations need to be open to new data and unexpected events, they lack the millennia required to consider every possible idea. They have to use a more systematic process. For our purposes, individuals and organizations must insert a third step between generation and testing: developing and evaluating the initial ideas.

Brainstorming, originated in the 1950s and then repopularized by the quality movement in the 1980s and 1990s, represents by far the most common method for generating new ideas, including new ideas for products and services. While brainstorming in its original and several modified forms helps to break the crust of established mind-sets up to a point, it doesn't include significant tools for the evaluation and development phase. Sadly, few organizations have effective methods for these phases, and in most organizations, evaluation and development end up being the property of R&D or product development. (3M is perhaps the clearest exception to this generalization, with an evaluation and development "system" that would drive most organizations up a wall—or head-on into it.)

Because they lack effective means for generating, evaluating and developing, and then testing ideas, all too many organizations OD quickly on even a limited selection of new ideas. Just as organizations limit ideas for their own products and services to a few specific departments, they avoid the need to deal with a variety of products and services used internally by creating internal monopolies to provide these goods and services: maintenance, administrative support, human relations systems, accounting and financial services, management information systems, and so on.

3. *Given traditional means of organization and operation, it costs far more to try out a new product, service, or idea than to reproduce or slightly modify an existing one.* The entire modern industrial enterprise, in every developed nation, is based on routinization of all possible processes. Chapter 2 dealt with this as the organizational system's attempt to minimize resource usage and seek

equilibrium. Given this goal, the more that a new product, service, or idea differs from an existing one, the more expensive it is to implement, even if the implementation is only a test.

Organizations can take specific steps to change this situation. Hewlett-Packard, for instance, has received continuing attention for its willingness to make its own products obsolete before its competitors can. GE creates new products using as much existing technology as possible, then further develops the products after they have hit the market. Rubbermaid used its reputation as a high-quality manufacturer of plastic products in a relatively narrow niche to become a company that currently markets an average of one new product a day in a variety of niches.

How do you organize so that you can still use routine processes where necessary, but develop the competence to create new ideas, products, and services economically? Read on.

4. *When managers accept internal free enterprise or democracy or both, it feels very much as if they're giving up control.* According to Deepak Chopra,[1] studies show that stress occurs in situations that are characterized by unpredictability, lack of control, and the inability to express frustration. He's probably right, because American industry has persistently attempted to control both its markets (producing predictability of demand) and its internal operations. And if one principle is deeply embedded in this same industry, it is the right of supervisors, managers, and executives to chew out their subordinates when they are frustrated. (This is not a joke. In the overwhelming majority of traditional, hierarchical organizations, to modify a well-known saying only slightly, stress rolls downhill.) And is it an accident that in a world where unpredictability and lack of control must be taken for granted, the popularity of the golden parachute (a substitute for predictability) has risen sharply?

Unfortunately, this need for predictability and control has consistently led organizations to stress control at the expense of productivity and innovation. Shoshona Zuboff, in *In the Age of the Smart Machine,* recounts the story of the pharmaceutical company that abolished its E-mail system not because it wasn't effective—it was—but because it could not control it. Barbara

Garson (*The Electronic Sweatshop*) was amazed at how often computer systems appeared to be implemented not to control costs or increase productivity but simply to control employees. In fact, despite the emphasis on using information systems to enhance revenue, it appears that the overwhelming majority of these systems exist to control both processes and employees and to provide control information.

How serious is this? While all effectively self-organizing systems depend on prompt, direct feedback, typical information systems provide feedback almost exclusively to the top levels of management. Since this level seldom makes operating decisions, the feedback rarely arrives in time or in enough detail to permit these managers to effectively improve operations with precision. Instead, their options are frequently limited to (1) making broad strategic changes, such as dropping product lines or selling off entire divisions; (2) increasing "pressure for results" on subordinate managers; or (3) making broadax decisions such as demanding employment cuts of 10 percent or mandating other forms of cost cutting. Meanwhile, these actions make life both less predictable and less controllable at the operating level—the level that most needs to be self-organizing.

In short, the emphasis on control, as practiced by the typical organization, makes effective self-organization all but impossible at the point where it's needed. Many of today's most progressive companies have recognized this, though no one has come up with a universal solution.

Replacing Internal Monopolies

Before we look at ways of implementing an internal free market in products, services, and ideas, we ought first to take a quick look at a ubiquitous feature of most organizations of any size: internal monopolies. These monopolies are designed to provide the specific services needed by the organization both efficiently and effectively. Like most monopolies, they seldom accomplish either mission well.

Two popularly discussed alternatives to these internal monopolies are outsourcing and creating "virtual corporations."

The third alternative, internal free enterprise, gets far less attention. Since this book advocates the third alternative, we need to look at the first two.

A currently popular solution to the inefficiency of internal monopolies is to outsource some of the services; maintenance of various kinds and information systems appear to be at the top of most lists, with sporadic outsourcing of other functions. When an organization signs a contract with an outsourcer, in effect it transfers the monopoly its internal activity enjoyed to an external activity. It keeps the same basic structure, but gives up some—and often significant—control over the activity. It assumes that the outsourcer, who specializes in that kind of work, will perform it more economically and relieve the organization of having to worry about it.

Standard outsourcing works best for "nonvalue-adding" (resourcing) activities. For instance, several corporations that initially outsourced the bulk of their computing have now taken back all but the operation and maintenance of established systems. The currently dwindling volume of new outsourcing contracts for management information systems concentrates on the same routine operations.

Another outsourcing method available to a company skilled at partnering is to outsource a variety of support operations to "best-in-class" providers. Hewlett-Packard, for instance, is busily exploring this option, as are numerous other companies. In theory, this means that the function is performed by the organization that can do it best.

Companies have too little experience with outsourcing, especially outsourcing to "best-in-class" suppliers, for us to draw many conclusions as yet. And this is true in spades of the second alternative: creating a "virtual corporation." Certainly virtual corporations have garnered significant press, having been featured in James Bryan Quinn's *Intelligent Enterprise* and William H. Davidow and Michael S. Malone's *The Virtual Corporation*, among others. But there is, so far, little data on which to evaluate their use outside of narrow niches. (Benetton, the most famous of the virtual corporations, has currently fallen on hard times. Will their virtualness help or hinder their attempt to come back? Perhaps you'll know by the time you read this.)

Why so hard-nosed in my evaluation of outsourcing? Am I trying to downplay these alternatives? Not at all. I just want to point out that although outsourcing and virtuality are much hyped, they have yet to prove themselves as effective substitutes for internal monopolies. Given this, perhaps it makes sense to consider a third alternative: internal free enterprise.

Implementing an Internal Market in Goods and Services

Most managers, academics, and top management people believe that an organization gets effective support by using essentially monopolistic internal sources. But neither outsourcing nor forming a virtual corporation deals with the fundamental problem: the monopoly itself. Both of them shift the problem off the organization's plate, but the provider remains a monopoly. And if two hundred years of history since Adam Smith have taught us anything, it is that monopoly—whether internal or external, outsourced or virtual—neither produces goods and services of relevant variety nor produces them at market prices. In short, you can goldplate it infinitely, but monopoly remains monopoly.

The following story is admittedly extreme, but some form of it could be repeated in virtually every large organization that depends on internal monopolies. Several years ago, a major New York bank found that its costs for overnight delivery services were skyrocketing. After appropriate investigation, it found that the increase had a simple cause: Workers were using overnight mail to get letters and packages from their floor to other floors, a service that the internal mail service, an "efficient" internal monopoly, wasn't able to perform. Don't think of this as an isolated example. My organization routinely uses overnight services for mail that doesn't really have to arrive until the second day. But we find that even Priority Mail, which goes through the mailroom at our end and then the mailroom at the other end, never arrives in less than four days.

Now it seems sensible to ask: Why not at least try an alternative? Instead of trying to grow wings on the monopoly pig, simply require the internal providers who furnish goods and services to your organization to operate in a true market economy. Let their customers buy from them or from external providers, whichever provides the best value. If you were to do this, how might you proceed? You might begin by gathering some data:

- First, recognize that unless you have spent considerable effort implementing a true "chain-of-customers" orientation, your internal monopoly providers are furnishing what they believe their customers *ought* to have, not necessarily what they *want*. The tendency of internal monopoly providers to furnish what they believe customers should have runs from the top to the bottom of the organization. You'll find it in the motor pool, your office supply operation, your maintenance operation, and even more so in "professional" functions like human resources, organizational development, and management information systems. If establishing an internal market economy did nothing more than force them to respond to real customer needs, which it will, your organization will, as they say, make out like a bandit. It will flush a great deal of expensive inefficiency out of the system. In our experience, this one benefit alone will justify whatever time and effort it takes to establish internal free enterprise.

- How much inefficiency is there, really? A recent ad by a firm in search of outsourcing contracts claimed that it took $100 worth of the time of seven people to buy a $7 hammer. Where did it get these statistics? I have no idea. But let's suppose that it actually takes only a third of the figure, $33, to buy that hammer. That's a tremendous amount of inefficiency. And it gives an outsourcer a tremendous cushion with which to offer you lower prices and still make a bundle for itself. Why the inefficiency? Because your organization created it, probably because it tried to combine resourcing with control in the same unit. When this happens, control invariably wins. An outsourcer can perform the same function more economically because it has no control responsibility. If you maintain the control responsibility internally, however, you may actually be paying just as much to get that hammer but hiding a significant part of the costs.[2]

▪ But wait—as the pitchman says—there's more! One of the shocks within the quality movement came when organizations discovered that a major cost of (poor) quality was the cost of "work-arounds"—the time, money, and effort that internal customers spend getting around the inefficiencies caused by their internal providers. All the games that units play to coax, appropriate, or coerce what they need. All the excuses they find to go around the providers. Look at any organization when it doesn't know you're looking, and you'll find that one of the most valuable workers is the one who knows how to bypass the system and get what's needed in a hurry. (Were you perhaps one of these people when you were on your way up? I was.)

If you can find a manager who will level with you and who knows what's going on, see what she really does to work around the inefficiencies. Or spend a little time to find out how many organizational development or human resources projects have been begun because a staff department sold them to a higher-level manager, not because operating managers requested them. Then look at the projects that were developed by similar staff offices and implemented by management decree, and determine how many of them are still operating to everyone's satisfaction at least three years after they were implemented. Hint: If you get honest answers, prepare to be shocked.

Now you have some data, and the data should kick-start your motivation because now you can see the problem that's been hiding under the cover of "efficiency" and "cost-effectiveness" for months, years, or even decades. Are you ready to act? When you do, keep clearly in mind that you are genuinely offering an opportunity to your internal providers as well as to their customers. You are *not* punishing them. Why should you? You're the one who's been wanting them to do just what they've been doing. Now you're going to change your expectations and help them to create far more responsive organizations.

Start looking at two groups of targets. One group will include routine operations, such as supply, maintenance, office machine repair, and administrative services. You should assign someone to start making them internal entrepreneurs. You concentrate on the second, more "knowledge work" group of operations, such as training, organization development, EEO, and safety.

What do you want done with the routine operations?

1. First, find the activities closest to those that are easily and widely available on the commercial market without a contract or through easily negotiated, short-term contracts. You're pursuing a simple goal at this point: identifying outside sources that can provide genuine competition to your internal providers without involving you in either extended contract negotiations or extended contracts.

2. Don't just look at internal activities and their functions, however. Look for activities led by strong, confident managers who will see operating in a free market as a challenge, not as a threat to be dodged at all costs. Believe me, these are not just words. You want to find a real entrepreneur, someone who will take the challenge and create a truly competitive organization out of the internal monopoly. He or she should also be an effective leader, because all too many individuals in the organization are going to see the process as a threat.

3. Now establish a date, at least six months in the future, after which the internal supplier's customers will be able to buy from whatever source they like. What happens during this period? If you've chosen rightly, at least two activities valuable to the organization as a whole. First, the internal provider will suddenly start listening very closely to its customers, at the same time that it learns what its competition is. Second, using this information, it will begin to change its operations. It may very well decide that it can't compete with certain products or services. It may significantly change how it provides others. It may begin to reduce its staff. When the target date comes, it's prepared to hit the ground running. From then on, it's on its own. Unless there's a compelling reason to keep the internal provider or part of it, it sinks or swims on the basis of its ability to compete with outside providers. On the whole, however, you want it to swim; just as you don't want to favor it, neither do you want to do anything to sabotage it.

You will get a payoff from making these internal suppliers compete. Prices to internal customers will go down. The relevance of the suppliers' offerings will rise. They will simply be more responsive. All these constitute real gains. But they're nothing to the gains you can get from enabling knowledge-based activities, the second group, to become entrepreneurial.

Look for a knowledge-work activity that's a significant cost center; you won't gain much if you choose a marginal operation with a low budget. Look at human resources, training, contracting, and any other high-level activity that is a provider to other internal organizations. Once again, look at the same time for a strong manager who'll jump at the chance to be entrepreneurial—and who'll convince her people that they should jump at the chance.

Don't count on making these kinds of activities entrepreneurial overnight. You don't want them to delay becoming entrepreneurial, but you'll ruin half the benefit if you try to force the situation on them without preparation. You might find this three-step process useful:

1. Identify the amount that each internal customer spends with this supplier over a year. Then "fence" this amount and provide at least six months but preferably an entire annual budget cycle in which the customer must spend this amount with the supplier, but can negotiate what the amount is spent for. This gives the customer a chance to start thinking about what it really wants and to develop a much clearer sense of what its needs really are. It gives the supplier the chance to start listening seriously to the customer and to try to develop products and services to meet that customer's needs. And it gives both suppliers and customers the chance to negotiate with one another in a way they've probably never negotiated before. It also gives your organization the chance to develop internal processes by which customers can contract with and pay internal suppliers. You may find that this is anything but a trivial matter. In my organization's case, it took eighteen months to find out how we could contract and collect for our services with our field locations.

2. As an optional second step, you may want to consider an additional one-year period during which the customer can de-

cide whether to purchase specific goods or services and what they are to be—but must purchase them only from the internal supplier. I don't recommend this in general, but if the supplier has the kind of low sensitivity that most operational managers associate with their suppliers, it may be necessary. While the step may appear to delay the process, you'll find that the supplier begins to wake up and make wholesale changes in the way it does business—and the customer begins to get products and services far more relevant to its needs.

3. Now take the final step: At the end of the time period, the funds formerly spent on the supplier simply become general funds available to the customer without restriction. Turn your internal customers loose to buy what they need whenever they need it. Does it sound as if chaos will ensue? Not if you've chosen the right supplier organization. It will be wheelin' and dealin' and focusing on its customers like you wouldn't believe.

It won't be all sweetness and light; there will be problems. You can count on two of these problems and be prepared to deal effectively with them.

1. Every organization treasures its unique "professional-ism." Your design engineers want to act like professionals; so do your systems designers and programmers, your procurement specialists and college recruiters. When you start talking of making them dependent on their customers' desires, you'll run into this professionalism in a big way. And if the function happens to have a legal basis, such as EEO or OSHA, its objection to letting customers dictate its activities will rise exponentially. Some justification exists for this resistance; organizations do have to follow the laws and regulations and maintain some internal standards. But these standards have to be balanced against, and if necessary take second place to, the needs of customers. Expect the resistance, understand it, but make it clear that while you expect undeviating compliance with the law, on other issues customers have the last word.

2. You and other senior managers may become the biggest obstacle to the success of your entrepreneurial suppliers. Letting

an internal organization run as if it were a private enterprise is a heady experience. If the supplier is at all worth its salt, it will discover this quickly, and its managers will be leading the parade. The unit will begin showing an independence you've never seen before. (This applies equally to the organization providing routine products or services.) You may feel that you have indeed lost control. In a very real sense, you will have. But there will be control, the most effective control of all—the willingness of customer units to pay only for what they need. You may need to restrain the suppliers from their wildest excesses, but for heaven's sake, don't stand in the way of their using their ingenuity to build up their business. After all, isn't that the goal of the process?

Internal Markets: The Lessons

First, remember that I am not advocating internal free enterprise in products, services, and ideas because it's "good" or "American" or for any other ideological reason. That is not the point here. Your organization should consider internal free enterprise because it will ensure it access to varied products and services that meet its needs *and* to the ideas it can use to establish and maintain a competitive advantage.

An internal free market in products and services produces a generally different result from an internal free market in ideas, and the two versions of the market complement each other. A true internal market economy in goods and services—which means that your internal suppliers compete with external suppliers at every point possible—will ensure that you get a relevant variety of these goods and services at a competitive cost. It will not ensure that these goods and services are innovative, because that depends on the innovativeness of the internal customers of these goods and services. This innovation results from the internal market in ideas. This market will produce a wide variety of ideas, and the best predictor of the effectiveness of an idea is the number of other ideas against which it has had to compete in order to survive. Then, properly organized, the market will develop and evaluate these ideas to the point where they can be successfully tested. In short, the combination of the two will enhance both effective self-organization and overall organizational success.

Biological evolution consists of the complementary processes of generating broad variety and then selecting the most adaptable individuals and species from among that variety. This chapter has presented some reasons why an internal free market in goods and services may be the best way for an organization to implement these processes, thereby coming up with the best alternatives from a variety of possibilities. Now we turn to ways of implementing an internal free market in ideas.

10

Punctuating the Equilibrium

Darwin thought that evolution proceeded smoothly, without big jumps. A new theory suggests that instead it proceeds by "punctuated equilibrium," in which periods of long stability are followed by periods of rapid change. Organizations can evolve most successfully when they understand and consciously use the basic mechanism of punctuated equilibrium.

Until just a few decades ago, most evolutionary biologists agreed with Darwin that most evolutionary change occurred in small steps. Then the science of paleontology found anything but smooth, incremental evolution in the fossil records. Many paleontologists and biologists now believe that species and the balance among them tended to remain stable for a long time, then suddenly changed. Old species changed or vanished and new species arose. A completely new balance came into existence. (Remember that *suddenly* in evolutionary language means millions of years.) The process is called punctuated equilibrium, and it remains one of the hot topics in evolutionary theory.

Can the idea of punctuated equilibrium be applied to organizations? It certainly seems to fit the currently popular model of "transformational" change. Or does it perhaps point in a completely different direction?

Sudden, Massive, Transformational Change

If we take a superficial look at the idea of punctuated equilibrium, we might conclude that the organizational form of it is rapid transformational change. An organization remains the same for years, often decades. Then suddenly it changes to a new and very different configuration. Xerox did it. Motorola did it. GM is trying and trying and trying to do it. Many academics and consultants seem to be proclaiming that transformational change is the only way to go.

In fact, this type of sudden, gut-wrenching change does occur in organizations, and occasionally it occurs successfully. But this is most definitely not what evolutionary theorists mean by punctuated equilibrium. In biological punctuated evolution, the change may *appear* sudden. However, the change has been percolating and spreading under the surface for a long time—for hundreds of thousands or even millions of years. When we look at organizations, a great deal of "sudden" change turns out to have this same characteristic: slow development within the organization for years, then its sudden entrance into the limelight.

Xerox is often held up as an example of a large organization that changed successfully. It did, and it did because its CEO, David Kearns, pushed the change for almost a decade. But there was something else interesting about the change. Kearns carefully seeded the organization with new ideas, letting them take root where they could. At the same time that he was attempting to change the organization from the top, many of the changes he wanted were bubbling up from the heart of the organization. And much of Motorola's well-known success began when workers and supervisors were trained in quality methods and began to apply them on the work floor. (Interestingly enough, though, this part of the change was seriously handicapped until higher-level managers were also trained so that they would understand and permit the change at the working level.)

Perhaps, then, we should look more closely at the basic idea of punctuated equilibrium—the idea that massive change at the center often begins as a series of smaller changes at the periphery.

Change Follows Information Flow

Paleontologist Steven Jay Gould helped originate, and remains a strong proponent of, the theory of punctuated equilibrium. He has a clear thesis: The "sudden" evolutionary change that punctuates the existing equilibrium begins on the fringe of a population. How does this happen? The central population remains relatively insulated from changes in the environment occurring around it, but smaller groups more or less isolated at the periphery feel the impact of them daily. As a result of this constant pressure, these small groups begin to evolve. Eventually, the new and better adapted versions at the periphery begin to percolate back through the population as a whole, replacing the former equilibrium of the group with a new and better adapted equilibrium.[1]

Gould's thesis remains somewhat speculative for biological evolution. For organizational evolution, however, the thesis is far less speculative. Many of the most important changes in organizations in fact occur at the fringes and only slowly begin to affect the organization as a whole. And this happens for many of the same reasons that Gould gives for punctuated equilibrium in biological evolution.

First, recall that stability and evolution both depend on information flow. Organizational systems remain stable in large part because they carefully filter the ideas and data available to them from the environment. The closer one gets to the center of the organization—the corporate staff and top management—the more complete the filtering process is. In part, this results from the nature of hierarchical organizations. Decades of research make it clear that data and ideas at odds with an organization's current beliefs move up the chain of command very, very slowly, presuming they manage to get into the formal information flow at all. Salespeople, dealers, repairers, and others in constant contact with actual and potential customers have their faces rubbed in the real world every day. In many organizations, so do those—editors, buyers, procurement agents—who must deal with suppliers. CEOs virtually never do.

Just as stability and change depend on the flow of information, information flow depends for its very definition on the purposes of the individuals who use it. Apart from some purpose, no facts are ever more than data and no idea is ever looked at twice. In looking at an organization, however, we need to refine the two divisions of "core" and "periphery" somewhat. We need to break the organization down into four general areas: the strategic core, the operating core, the customer-supplier interface, and the resource component. The customer-supplier interface is basically the organization's periphery—although there is nothing peripheral about relationships with either customers or suppliers. And in an organization, the definition of what should comprise the information flow changes dramatically as we move from one area to another:

1. *At the strategic core,* the information flow contains ideas and data that relate directly to the organization's performance in regard to its strategic plan, its core business, its profit objectives, its stockholder value, and similar global issues.
2. *At the operating core,* the information flow is made up of ideas and data that relate directly to the quality, timeliness, effectiveness, and efficiency of the internal productive processes of the organization.
3. *At the customer-supplier interface,* the information flow consists of ideas and data that enable salespeople, maintainers and repairers, customer service personnel, buyers, and their kin to react quickly and successfully to their requirements as either customers or suppliers.
4. *In the resource component,* the information flow is focused on ideas and data pertaining to developing programs for, exercising control over, and furnishing goods and services to the other parts of the organization.

These four general areas define the ideas and data that will become part of an organization's information flow in very different ways. They also focus on the available ideas and data in two very different ways. First, customer-supplier and operating concerns are essentially real-time (what can I do to solve this problem today?), whereas strategic concerns and most resourcing concerns are focused on the present only insofar as it relates to established plans and strategies (how are we doing against our plans?). Second, customer-supplier and operating concerns tend to be very specific (what do I need to do for this customer, supplier, or process?), while strategic concerns are far broader (what do we need to do to serve this market better?). Resource component concerns tend to be a mix of the two.

It's no wonder that new ideas and data are forced onto such a long and tortuous path as they attempt to move among the strategic core, the operating core, the customer-supplier interface, and the resource component. They must survive shifts in focus, in time constraints, and in degree of detail. It appears almost as if what constitutes information in one area becomes little more than noise when it reaches another area. "Market penetration," a key strategic concern, may be noise to a salesperson trying to fulfill this quarter's quota, utterly meaningless in the operating core except as it affects production, and irrelevant to the resource component except for the marketing division. "Quality" means one thing to marketing (part of the resource component), something else to manufacturing (in the operating core), and still another thing to customer service and procurement (at the customer-supplier interface). As a way of visualizing this process, look at Figure 1.

You may be far more used to thinking in terms of customers than of suppliers. If I want to buy an off-the-shelf desktop computer, I have a wide variety of suppliers to choose from. I need not worry a lot about my relationship with any individual supplier. On the other hand, if I need an efficient parallel-processing system and need to remain close to the state of the art, my universe of suppliers is small indeed. My best interests are served by developing close relationships with the few companies that build high-powered parallel-processing machines, perhaps even by partnering closely with one of them. In other words, depending on your business, relationships with suppliers may be at least as important as relationships with customers. This is heresy, perhaps, but a real-world fact.

Figure 1's diagram of an organization appears very similar to the one most of us grew up with—a pyramid with the workers at the bottom, the staff in the middle, and top management

Figure 1. The four areas of organization.

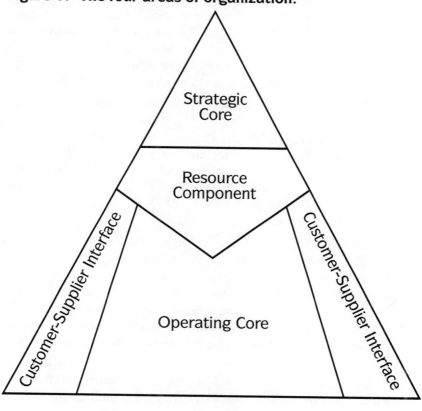

at the top. Certainly it can be viewed this way. And in the traditional pyramid, so management theory held, direction moved down from the top while information moved up from the bottom.

In fact, that understanding of organization is seriously flawed for today's competitive environment, as managers have begun to realize. When an organization of any size tries to operate on the basis of the traditional model in today's world, it finds that:

▪ *The individuals who form the strategic core cannot possibly acquire and use enough information to make anything but the broadest strategic decisions.* In the four decades after World War II, organizations attempted to compensate for this by creating ever larger staff departments to gather this information and to make recommendations to the strategic core. By the late 1980s, it began to be obvious that this arrangement couldn't deal with a highly competitive global environment, and organizations accordingly began to downsize their central staffs, sometimes wholesale.

■ *The staff offices preempted the information function, so that all information that reached the strategic core was either gathered by or filtered through them.* We've already seen that each layer and each function filters information for its own purposes as it passes through. Consequently, the information fed the strategic core was overwhelmingly what it expected to hear—and given the appropriate spin to make the staff offices look good (another reason for downsizing).

■ *The core of the traditional model is based on the practices of such institutions as the Roman Catholic Church and the Prussian and other armies, which do not in any meaningful sense have customers.* Consequently, American organizations took a long time—over a century—to accept the critical role of the customer. It took the same length of time to realize that the interface between the organization and its customers (and suppliers) was also critical.

Why belabor these points? Because the traditional model of organization exemplifies one extreme of the biological concept of punctuated evolution. An isolated central population—the strategic core supported by its staff offices—maintains its integrity. Evolutionary changes occurring at the customer-supplier interface seldom make an impact on this central population. Therefore, as the changes in the environment make the strategy of the central population less and less relevant, the result tends to be a wholesale shake-up in the organization and its top management. It was unthinkable a few years ago that either IBM or Kodak would even consider selecting a complete outsider as CEO. But each did, because the strong culture of the strategic core and the staff offices supporting it continually rejected both data and ideas that would have forced it to change.

Note that this is an information problem. In biological evolution, the peripheral populations evolve because of environmental pressures on them, and this pressure is a form of information. In an organization, activities at the customer-supplier interface feel this same sort of pressure. Here the role of information is even clearer, as in "customers just don't like the new policies because they're potentially more expensive." When new ideas and data are confined to this interface, the discontinuity between the environment and the strategic core grows. If the situation lasts long enough, it produces an extreme form of punctuated equilibrium.

No one wants an organization that gets "punctuated" every few years. The alternative is an organization that can move new ideas and data from the customer-supplier interface to the operating and strategic cores quickly and then use this information to evolve successfully. This is the only real base on which an organization can "reinvent" itself successfully.

First, Get in the Race

How do you construct and operate an organization that is open to the ideas and data it needs to operate and evolve effectively? If you implement an internal free market, you will automatically make the boundaries between activities in the resource component and their internal customers much more open. Information on customer needs will flow much more freely into the resource component, resulting in far greater responsiveness on its part.

By the way, we might ask quickly, What makes up the resource component? The answer is every part of the organization that isn't setting strategy and integrating the operations of the organization in pursuit of this strategy (strategic core), creating products and services (operating core), or interfacing with customers or suppliers (the customer-supplier interface). Alternatively put, the resource component is made up of all activities that do not directly add value to the final customer. Does this make marketing, legal services, or strategic planning part of the resource component? It certainly does. Their nature as resources has been hidden by the fact that their customers, primarily the strategic core, can tell them what to do. But if they aren't seen as resources, supporting the activities that do directly add value, one needs to ask what in the world they do.

Back to the information flow. An internal free market helps open up this flow between the resource component and its internal customers. Having individuals from any area meet with individuals from other areas will also help open up the information flow between the areas. What else can an organization do, on a systematic basis, to create an information flow powerful enough to keep it from falling back into an extreme form of punctuated equilibrium? Here are six suggestions:

1. *The organization must intend to have a free information flow of new data and ideas from its environment and must intend the same free information flow within the organization and among its different areas.* Any effective management action begins with constant intent. An organization that intends to use self-organization and punctuated equilibrium to its advantage intentionally positions itself to get and circulate new ideas and data. It develops and improves whatever processes it needs to accomplish this. It takes account of it in all its decisions.

Executives and managers (like you) who lead an organization that intends to be open to ideas and information *will:*

- *Freely share information*—even information that might generate fear, anger, or other negative feelings. They mitigate these feelings by furnishing complete information and asking for reaction and feedback. For instance, managers will let members of the organization know if they are thinking of "rightsizing," will explain the reasons for such an action, and will ask for input on how it might be modified or avoided.
- *Be constantly responsive to new ideas and data.* They will not necessarily say, "That's a great idea—let's do it." But they will consistently say, "That may have some potential. Let's look at it more closely." Then they will ensure that it is in fact looked at more closely.
- *Treat new ideas, new data, and their bearers with respect.* When a new idea arises, they will ensure that it is looked at quickly and that the individual who presented it learns

the results of the initial look and of any subsequent actions that may be taken.

- *Make it crystal clear to all managers that soliciting and facili-*
tating ideas from their reports is a basic part of their job. Rate
them on this, of course. But don't ask for reports; that's an
invitation to game the system. Simply see to it that you
ask them as often as is necessary how they're doing at
getting ideas, and then stop and listen to what they say.
That communicates your intent clearly.

- *Try to find ways to implement as many ideas as possible, partic-*
ularly in the beginning. They won't implement poor ideas
or play games. If the idea has any promise at all, they will
help the originating individual to develop it. They will
keep in mind the impact on workers of the slogan used by
one organization: "We implement more than 85 percent
of all ideas we receive."

These executives and managers will *never:*

—tell anyone that the idea or fact presented isn't really in
his or her area of concern.

—suggest to an individual that he has more important
things to do than come up with ideas or pass along unexpected
data. Occasionally, an individual will attempt to make a career
out of new ideas. If the ideas have true potential, then pay him
or her to do just that. If they're not consistently that good, this is
a matter for a supervisor-performer discussion. But the situation
is never dealt with effectively by simply discouraging ideas.

2. *The organization should focus its information flow on the ideas*
and data most relevant to its strategic goals and their supporting objec-
tives, but never reject ideas or data simply because they don't clearly
fit these goals. At one extreme, an organization can reject any new
ideas or data not completely consistent with its current operations and strategy. But it can also go to the other extreme by
being so open to any and all new ideas and data that it has no
effective way to select from among them. An organization will
be most effective when it takes a middle course, guiding the
process toward important areas but not rejecting even the most
"off the wall" ideas.

Executives and managers who lead an organization that focuses ideas and data on key goals but never rejects other ideas *will:*

- *Constantly communicate the mission, shared values, goals, and objectives of the organization.* This means that organization members at every level understand the basic mission and strategy of the organization and how what they do fits in, and that they can identify the information and ideas most relevant both to them and to the larger organization.
- *Make clear that the basic goal of new ideas and data is to increase the organization's value to its customers and suppliers.* Everyone expects the question: "How might this help us create value for our organization by creating more value for our customers or suppliers?" And everyone with a new idea should be able to answer this question, even if the answer is only tentative at the start.
- *Use both formal and informal methods to emphasize those areas in which new ideas will be most helpful and to get detailed information on the specific ideas that will be most useful.* They will also ensure that members of the organization understand why these areas are important and how they can help the organization identify related ideas. They will also spend time simply wandering around and talking with people, asking them what they need. A new product or distribution method? A new sales emphasis? A way to reliably identify high-potential performers? And they will use the company paper to solicit information on areas where people most need ideas.
- *Look first for areas that are open to quick, significant improvement and communicate these clearly throughout the organization.* If the marketing department is one of the best, they accept ideas on how to improve it, but they don't concentrate on that area. If college recruiting is off, they may especially solicit ideas on how to turn that around.

These executives and managers will *never:*

—respond initially to new ideas or new data, no matter how irrelevant they might seem, with the statement that they have nothing to do with the organization's key issues. When an individual's ideas and/or data are rejected initially, no matter how considerate the rejection is, his willingness to contribute begins to seep away.

3. *Both ideas and data often appear in the context of a problem, but the organization should focus not on the problem but on the opportunities within it.* A key characteristic of people who excel at solving problems is this: They "look through" the problem to the opportunity within it, then seize that opportunity. Organizations deal most effectively with new ideas and data when they look at them as opportunities masquerading as problems.

Executives and managers who lead an organization that intends to focus on the opportunities hidden within problems *will*:

- *Listen carefully for the opportunities contained within any problems that arise.* For instance, "We lost 5 percent of market share this last quarter" could be heard as "Here's a chance to look at how the market is changing" or "Here's an invitation to reexamine our overall marketing strategy." "What do we have to do to restore our market share or at least cut our losses?" is perhaps the least opportunistic way of understanding the problem.
- *Encourage everyone else to do the same.* Ideally, each individual will present both the problem and the opportunity contained within it (never just the opportunity, because this would tie the organization to this one perception). While problems need to be translated into opportunities, the organization learns the most if it always has a clear view of the problem.
- *Mentor individuals on how to see through problems to opportunities.* Formal training in this can help, but the bottom line is the individual's ability to consistently identify hidden opportunities. By spending time fostering this ability in others, managers demonstrate their support for the entire process of idea and information flow. A strong mentoring relationship can also provide needed emotional support when an idea that an individual deeply believes in fails to be implemented.

These executives and managers will *never*:

—*criticize an individual for his or her inability to see an opportunity hidden within a problem.* Instead, the manager will use the occasion to help that individual develop skills at finding opportunities.

4. *The organization should expect everyone to tell it like it is—and expect everyone to ask the questions necessary to find out how it is. Honesty and openness are key values.* Despite pounds of value and vision statements, honesty and openness seldom comprise core values in most organizations. Not making mistakes (or at least not getting blamed for them), not offending key people, not causing problems, and similar self-protective behavior tend to be far more common—and useful—than honesty and openness. Unfortunately, such self-protective values go with rich new information and ideas like snowstorms go with sunbathing. You will almost certainly find it difficult to create and maintain an organization that does in fact reward honesty and openness. But you will find it virtually impossible to create an organization that values new ideas and information that is not open and honest.

Executives and managers who lead an organization that genuinely holds honesty and openness as key values *will:*

- *Demonstrate honesty and openness with each other and with everyone in the organization.* This means that the entire organization will learn effective conflict-resolution methods and routinely practice them. However, executives and managers will continually take the lead and model the performance they expect. How do you do this? You do it by "walking your talk," by being who you really are, saying what you really mean, and doing exactly what you say you'll do.
- *Ensure that each manager and every other individual not only expects honesty and openness but actively solicits and rewards it.* As part of this, individuals expect to keep their commitments and hold others to theirs. Everyone must see that these values actually work in the organization.

These executives and managers will *never:*

—lie.

—think, or suggest to anyone else, that in *this* particular situation other factors must take precedence over honesty and openness. Because there are so many reasons for being dishonest, a single instance of dishonesty can wreck an organization as surely as a single cancer can destroy a human body. Honesty is a harsh and demanding mistress.

—ask someone else to dissemble for any reason.

5. *The organization should consider its customers and suppliers as part of both its information flow and its decision-making processes.* As I write these words, "partnering" with customers and suppliers is one of the hot topics of the day. Good. But not so good unless the organization has developed real skill at partnering, which is not an easily gained skill. It is, however, a necessary one. If organizations want a continuing supply of high-quality ideas and data, making customers and suppliers part of the process pays dividends that can be found nowhere else.

How you partner and with whom are also important. Most customers and suppliers cannot reliably suggest major jumps forward or completely new products; they are too tied to their present operations. To get this level of new ideas, you must seek out the most imaginative customers and suppliers and work constantly with them to "jump out of the box" and find the genuinely new.

Executives and managers who lead an organization that considers both customers and suppliers as part of its idea and information flow and its decision-making process *will:*

- *Develop partnering skills at a very high level in the organization.* These skills can ultimately be delegated down to the appropriate levels, but they must begin at the top levels. First, the organization has to learn how to relate well with both its customers and suppliers. Then it has to progress beyond this to true partnering. The key: You have created a true partnering relationship only when each organization recognizes that the other is essential to its welfare and each can trust the other to concern itself with both organizations' welfare. But don't expect a partner ever to put your interest before its own. The partnership will function as long as, and to the extent that, both partners derive a clear benefit from it.
- *Expect every relationship with supplier partners and customer partners to be fully reciprocal.* Partnerships, like modern

marriages, last only when both parties get more from the relationship than they could get apart from it. While the relationship lasts, however, both parties take responsibility for both sides of it.

- *Understand that partnering is a dramatically different relationship from the traditional customer-supplier relationship.* When two companies enter into a partnering relationship, they give up the arm's-length relationship that characterizes traditional customer-supplier transactions and make commitments to each other that cannot quickly or lightly be dissolved. Thus honesty and openness become as important to this relationship as they are to relationships within the organization.

These executives and managers will *never:*

—attempt this demanding relationship without carefully evaluating its benefits and drawbacks and carefully developing the organizational skills required to support it.

6. *The organization needs to promote ownership and entrepreneurship everywhere.* Nothing kills an individual's willingness to generate ideas more effectively than taking his or her idea and giving it to someone else to develop. Important as the internal free market is, the underlying force of entrepreneurship from which it springs is even more important. And just as only individuals can change and only individuals can self-organize, so entrepreneurship within an organization ultimately depends on the willingness and ability of the individuals in that organization to think and act entrepreneurially—and on the opportunity given them for doing so. If they do not do so individually, the organization cannot do so at any higher level.

Executives and managers who lead an organization that promotes entrepreneurship and ownership of ideas *will:*

- *Take seriously the notion that individuals who originate ideas have an ownership stake in them.*
- *Create processes to ensure that individuals who come up with new ideas continue to be involved in their development.* How? At one extreme, the individual could be given the facilities and staff to lead the development effort. At the other, the individual might simply be part of a team responsible for

the development. And dozens of alternatives exist between the two extremes.[2]

These executives and managers will *never:*

—consider claiming someone else's idea as their own.

—be drawn into a "my people's ideas are better than your people's ideas" turf and status battle with each other.

Then Go for the Gold

We're approaching the finish line. To use the basic process of punctuated equilibrium while avoiding its most extreme form, the organization has opened all its boundaries to new ideas and data. Now it must process these ideas and data efficiently and effectively.

First, it finds that when it opens itself to a wide variety of new data and ideas, it opens itself to continuing potential distractions and perhaps even to a certain chaos. Ideas take time and effort to discover and present. They take additional time, effort, and money—sometimes great amounts of them—to develop and evaluate. Those that survive to the next stage must be tested and then, if all has gone well, implemented, which costs more time, effort, and money.

How can you, as manager, reconcile this "information overhead" with the necessity to produce a product or service at a competitive price? How do you keep the organization producing efficiently when ideas and data are whizzing around like so many bullets on an obstacle course? And not all those ideas will succeed. Not all will be worth implementing. More seriously, not all that can be implemented should be. Many ideas deserve to perish before significant time and effort are spent on them. Others, with real potential, need to be shelved for the time being and revisited later on. How does the organization deal with these issues?

To begin with, it doesn't start by framing the issues in this way, which would virtually guarantee that the flow of ideas will be damped. Instead, it asks: How can we concentrate organizational energies on the ideas with the greatest potential? If the organization does this, and makes certain that concentrating on high-potential ideas is both interesting and rewarding, people will have the time to work on the best ideas—and won't have the time to work on the other, less valuable ones.

How does it concentrate time and attention on high-potential ideas? Too few organizations make use of it, but there's a simple way to sort ideas—and data that may require new ideas—at every stage of development. Just ask these four key questions:

1. If successful, would this idea result in a product or service that will enhance the organization's revenue? That is, would it be of enough value to customers that the company could make a profit from offering it? If it has that potential, you have a Gold idea. Work it. Work it before working anything but another Gold idea or a Silver idea with exceptional potential. If you have so many Gold ideas that you don't have time to work on anything else, congratulate yourself. You're in the best competitive position possible.

2. If not a Gold idea, would it at least permit the organization to reduce the costs of delivering a product or service, without reducing the value of that offering to the customer? This is a Silver idea. Not so valuable as a Gold idea normally—who wants a Silver Medal if he can get a Gold one?—but one with clear value, nevertheless. Work it with whatever time remains from Gold ideas. Work it before even considering any Bronze ideas.

3. If not a Silver idea, would it at least indirectly support the goals of Gold or Silver ideas? This is a Bronze idea. If so, work it if there are no Gold or Silver ideas to work. That's a problem, because if there are no Gold or Silver ideas to work, the organization isn't generating the ideas it needs to compete and evolve successfully.

4. Finally, if not at least a Bronze idea, would it enable the organization to implement a currently fashionable idea and/or make some department or team's work easier, more interesting, or more up-to-date? It doesn't matter because this is a Lead idea, and it will of a certainty weigh the organization down for little or no benefit. Toss it—after a clear, considerate mentoring dis-

cussion with the individual who introduced it that helps you reach a consensus as to why it should be set aside.

These questions should indeed sound simple and logical to you. Actually, they're not quite the right questions. To be really successful, an organization needs to modify them slightly, and a quick look at the modifications will tell you why the second versions have more power. Here are the four questions again:

1. If successful, would the idea result in a product or service that would enhance the organization's revenue? That is, would it be of enough value to customers that the company could make a profit from offering it? If it has that potential, you have a Gold idea. Work it. Work it before working anything but another Gold idea or a Silver idea with exceptional potential. If you have so many Gold ideas that you don't have time to work on anything else, congratulate yourself. You're in the most competitive position possible.

2. If not a Gold idea, would it at least permit the organization to reduce the costs of delivering a product or service, without reducing the value of that offering to the customer? If yes, you have a Silver idea. But don't stop with this answer. Ask a second question: Can the idea be reworked to increase the value to customers at the same time that it reduces costs? Yes? Now you have another Gold idea to work. No? Then work it with whatever time remains from Gold ideas. Work it before working any Bronze Medal ideas. But keep looking to see if there's a way to upgrade it to a Gold idea.

3. If not a Silver idea, would it at least indirectly support the goals of Gold or Silver ideas? If yes, you have a Bronze idea. But don't stop with this answer. Ask a second question: Can the idea be reworked to decrease costs or even increase value to customers? Yes? Now you have at least a Silver idea to work. No? Then work it with whatever time remains from Gold and Silver ideas. If you work it, keep looking for Silver or Gold potential. If you work it, though, remember that it poses a problem, because if there are no Gold or Silver ideas to work, the organization isn't generating the ideas it needs to compete and evolve successfully.

4. Finally, if not at least a Bronze idea, would it enable the organization to implement a currently fashionable idea and/or make some department or team's work easier, more interesting, or more up-to-date? On those grounds, it's a Lead idea, and it will of a certainty weigh the organization down for little or no benefit. But take a look to see if there's a way to upgrade it at least to a Silver idea. If so, work it as one. If not, toss the idea—but only after a clear, considerate mentoring discussion with the individual who introduced it that helps you reach a consensus as to why it should be set aside and how he or she can produce at least a Silver Medal idea next time. (You will occasionally want to develop and evaluate a Bronze idea, but treat them as loss leaders. The organization needs to keep everyone's focus on Gold and Silver. How many times do you think that Greg Louganis's coach said to him: "Go after it today, son—get that Bronze Medal!").

Engrave this hierarchy of ideas, or your version of it, in the mind of every organization member. Put placards around that contain it. Make it the screen saver for all your PCs. Use it in all discussions and all awards. All self-organization, all effective performance, begins with clear goals. Where new ideas are concerned, these are the goals. Go!

Then Do It

Your organization has institutionalized its framework for soliciting ideas: revenue enhancement, cost control, then any others there might be surplus time for. Now, how do you establish a workable process for developing and evaluating the ideas, then testing and implementing the best one? Let me suggest guidelines, each making maximum use of self-organization:

1. Put the authority to develop, evaluate, and test the idea as close as possible to the working level that would implement it.
2. Put the authority to develop, evaluate, and test the idea in the smallest group possible.

3. Give the person who came up with the idea a clear stake in its success or failure.
4. Find a balance for your organization between giving free rein to idea development and getting the work out the door.

Let's refocus and look at each point in a little more detail.

1. Put the authority to develop, evaluate, and test the idea as close as possible to the working level that would implement it.

If you're serious about new ideas, you want the idea developed and evaluated as quickly as possible. The more layers of hierarchy it has to survive, the longer the process will take and the less likely the idea is to survive.

We started with the idea of punctuated equilibrium from evolutionary biology, in which new species develop at the periphery of the parent species' territory, then spread back through the parent species. We want ideas to follow the same path in our organization, and for this to happen, the ideas need to be developed and evaluated as close to origin as possible. To the extent that they must travel to a different area (operational core, strategic core, customer-supplier interface, and/or resource component), they will be (1) delayed, (2) given a neutral to hostile reception, or (3) simply ignored because there are more important things to do. So move ideas quickly into the self-organized work group or team that can use them and give this unit wide authority to develop, evaluate, and test them. And if the idea concerns only this group, give it the authority to implement it fully.

This, by the way, is not some blue-skies idea. Ford used this approach to design the original Taurus and then to design its 1996 makeover. Chrysler used it to produce a string of high-style cars, from the LH series to the Cirrus. And hundreds of other companies, who don't get the publicity, use it successfully to generate new products and services.

If you're serious about using self-organization and new ideas to create and maintain competitive advantage, see that development, evaluation, and testing occur where the action is—not where people spend most of their workdays, wondering what the action should be.

2. Put the authority to develop, evaluate, and test the idea in the smallest group possible.

The more individuals required to reach a decision on an idea, the longer it takes and the less likely it is to survive. Why? Because the larger the group, the greater the probability is that one or more members will (1) delay considering the idea, (2) not really care about it, or (3) simply ignore it because there are more important things to do. On paper, self-organized teams can be as large as you want. In the real world, a self-organized team with more than eight to ten members will either work as two or more subteams or a smaller group within the team will be the real team and the rest will be hangers-on.

Clearly, the solution calls for a small, fast, creative self-organizing team, quite possibly a multifunctional one. Perhaps you need to set up teams like this just to develop, evaluate, and test new ideas. Do it, but keep them as close to the action as possible. Don't let them gravitate higher in the organization—which they will almost certainly try to do. High-level, high-status units divorced from day-to-day work and assigned to a high level in the organization are one of the most effective idea assassins known to either man or woman. Far more serious, they are also one of the greatest generators of Bronze and Lead ideas that you could wish for—for your competitors.

Neither Ford nor Chrysler's product-development multifunctional teams are "small" in this sense. But they are small when compared with the nonteam organizations they replaced. And all large teams such as these work through a series of subteams, many of them preserving the multifunctional structure of the parent team.

3. Give the person who came up with the idea a clear stake in its success or failure.

Points 1 and 2 above suggested how an idea gets short-changed if it has to move through several layers or a large number of people. Even when the path is short and the group small, however, few people share the enthusiasm of the individual who came up with it. So give this individual as much involvement in and authority over its development as possible.

There's another facet to this, one that hasn't been stressed so far. Hand in hand with this opportunity, however, goes a responsibility. The organization needs to reward effective ideas but at the same time protect itself from overenthusiasm—by giving the individual a clear stake in either the success or failure of the idea. Remember, entrepreneurs fail, and the good ones learn from their failures. You're supporting profitable risk taking. You are not supporting playing with interesting ideas. Universities do that and call it research.

Let me repeat myself one more time. If possible, especially if the idea looks like a high potential Gold one, let its originator manage its development, evaluation, and testing. If that's not possible, come as close to that goal as possible.

4. Find a balance for your organization between giving free rein to idea development and getting the work out the door.

Ah, now we've reached the point where the radials meet the potholes. How do you balance new ideas and the time they take against the cold, hard fact that customers pay only for delivered goods and services? Sad to relate, this question has no one-size-fits-all answer. 3M doesn't balance work load and new ideas the way that Rubbermaid or Compaq or Apple do, and you probably can't balance the two in the same way that any of them do.

Here's a suggestion, though: Find a company in an industry close to your own, but one that doesn't compete with you, and use the well-established technique of benchmarking. Don't, *don't* get involved in the administrative niceties of benchmarking; you may actually be better off if you haven't done it before. Just get the right people in your organization talking with the right people in their organization. Then perform high-level brain-picking.

These suggestions will help you implement an organization that avoids the worst form of punctuated equilibrium, the form that results in stagnation followed by wholesale change at every level. The more you can create an open, effective flow of ideas, the more you will move your organization from an equilibrium-seeking, stable system to one that is complex, adaptive, and seldom stable. You may not feel that you have the control you had before, but you will have an organization that will not be punctuated dramatically and traumatically every few years.

Epilogue: The Living Heart of the Process

We have taken a quick excursion through some key ideas drawn from biological evolution and examined how they might usefully be applied to make organizations more competitive in a dynamic world. We have looked at:

- the key ideas of biological evolution: generation of a wide variety of new possibilities through mutation and then selection of the most successful from this variety;
- the difficulty of "transformational" change in biological organisms and in organizations, and the fact that ultimately only individuals can change;
- the tendency of both organisms and organizations to seek niches they can dominate, thus leading them to equilibrium followed by entropy;
- the tendency of the internal components of an organizational system—technology, processes, functions and organizational structures, incentives, and competence—to maintain their integrity, that is, to resist change;
- the critical importance of information flow and of the knowledge and information embodied in an organization's culture for its evolution;
- the way in which subordinate organizational units also limit and sometimes drive the overall organization's evolution;
- the fact that all evolution is actually the *co*evolution of multiple organisms or organizations and how this makes the future course of evolution always unpredictable;

- the necessity for self-organization as the basis of all organization;
- the effectiveness of an internal free market as a way of producing variety and providing effective selection methods; and
- the biological idea of punctuated equilibrium—based on information flow—that an organization can use to prevent sudden, traumatic change.

I hope that these ideas get you to thinking and that you implement some of the suggestions based on them. But this is the final thought I'd like to leave with you:

Only individuals change, and they change by making choices. In both the long and short runs, all "organizational" change is the sum of the changes made by the individuals in the organization, and each individual will change (or not) based on how the change affects his or her individual purposes.

To succeed, all theory and practice of organizational change must take account of this simple, often overlooked fact.

Notes

Chapter 1

1. Alan L. Wilkins, *Developing Corporate Character: How to Successfully Change an Organization Without Destroying It* (San Francisco: Jossey-Bass, 1989), p. 8.
2. H. Dan Lemke, "Open: What's Important in Today's EDI and Computer Systems," *EDI World*, July 1994, pp. 28–29. Lemke makes one mistake in his statement: He treats enhancing quality as something different from generating new services for customers and reducing costs. In fact, companies with the most effective quality programs are able to simultaneously increase customer value and reduce costs.
3. Kenichi Ohmae, *The Mind of the Strategist: Business Planning for Competitive Advantage* (New York: Viking Penguin, 1983), p. 224.
4. Ibid., p. 227.
5. Henry Mintzberg deals with this at length in *The Rise and Fall of Strategic Planning* (New York: Free Press, 1994), pp. 227–245. On page 245, he makes the telling comment: "In our own studies, situations sometimes remained roughly stable for decades, only to collapse in a period of weeks."
6. Tom Peters, *The Pursuit of WOW!* (New York: Vintage, 1994), p. 61.

Chapter 2

1. See Michael Treacy and Fred Wiersema, *The Discipline of Market Leaders* (Reading, Mass.: Addison-Wesley, 1995), pp. 2–3.

2. "It Looks Like a PC Maker, Walks Like a PC Maker . . . ," *Business Week,* Dec. 12, 1994, p. 106.
3. Paul Ingrassia and Joseph B. White, *Comeback: The Fall & Rise of the American Automobile Industry* (New York: Simon and Schuster, 1994), p. 15.

Chapter 3

1. For more information, see Erich Jantsch, *The Self-Organizing Universe* (Oxford: Pergamon, 1980), p. 140.
2. For more detail on the importance of eukaryotic cells, see John Sepkioski, "Foundations: Life in the Oceans," in *The Book of Life,* Stephen Jay Gould, ed. (New York: W. W. Norton, 1993), pp. 37–64, esp. pp. 44–45.
3. Mihaly Csikszentmihalyi, Kevin Rathunde, Samuel Whalen, with contributions by Maria Wong, *Talented Teenagers: The Roots of Success and Failure* (New York: Cambridge University Press, 1993), pp. 12–13.
4. Erich Jantsch, *The Self-Organizing Universe,* p. 7.
5. Peter Senge, *The Fifth Discipline: The Art & Practice of the Learning Organization* (New York: Doubleday, 1990), p. 58.

Chapter 4

1. I devoted Chapter 3 of my book *The Competitive Power of Constant Creativity* (New York: AMACOM, 1994) to an in-depth examination of these unstated assumptions, which I referred to there as "frames."
2. The first book to present Dr. Csikszentmihalyi's findings was *Beyond Boredom and Anxiety* (San Francisco: Jossey-Bass, 1977). He summarized these findings and included others in a more popular work, *Flow* (New York: Harper & Row, 1990). His most recent book, *The Evolving Self* (New York: HarperCollins, 1993), relates his findings specifically to biological evolution.
3. Ingrassia and White, p. 39.

Chapter 6

1. For an example of the application of game theory, see "Businessman's Dilemma," an interview with Barry Nalebuff by Rita Koselka in *Forbes* magazine, Oct. 11, 1993, pp. 107–109.

2. This specific information was taken from Jaclyn Fierman, "Winning Ideas From Maverick Managers," *Fortune* magazine, February 6, 1995, pp. 66–80. Jack Stack has described his approach in much more detail in *The Great Game of Business* (New York: Doubleday/Currency, 1992).

Chapter 7

1. Stephen Jay Gould, "The Evolution of Life on the Earth," *Scientific American*, October 1994, pp. 85–86.
2. Gary McWilliams, "At Compaq, a Desktop Crystal Ball," *Business Week*, March 20, 1995, pp. 96–97.
3. Paraphrased from the first chapter of *The Competitive Power of Constant Creativity*.

Chapter 8

1. I am, once again, indebted to Anthony Putman, president of Descriptive Systems, Ann Arbor, Mich., who pointed out the basic truth of self-organization to me.
2. To be fair, not all studies during the same period yielded the same results. The argument persists until today on two fronts: (1) Do employers need more highly skilled high-school graduates for their jobs, and (2) if not, would they upgrade jobs and use the higher skills if they were available?

Chapter 9

1. On tape one, side two of his tape *Ageless Body, Timeless Mind*.
2. While there's no time to deal with the fatal tendency of organizations to push control responsibilities onto internal resource providers, it absolutely guarantees that the provider will be "bureaucratic." For a humorous but helpful presentation of the problem, see Dirk Cjelli, "PT Confronts the Primary Bureaucratic Dysfunction," *Performance & Instruction*, August 1992, pp. 5–7.

Chapter 10

1. For a more specific exposition of this, see Stephen Jay Gould's *The Panda's Thumb* (New York: Norton, 1980), pp. 183–184.

2. *The Competitive Power of Constant Creativity* contains an extended discussion of supporting entrepreneurship and of the roles that individuals who initiate ideas can play in their subsequent development.

Bibliography

Beer, Michael, Russell A. Eisenstat, and Bert Spector. "Why Change Programs Don't Produce Change." *Harvard Business Review,* November–December 1990, pp. 158–66.

————. *The Critical Path to Corporate Renewal.* Boston: Harvard Business School Press, 1990. If you still believe that programmatic change ("Lets do TQM") works, read at least the article and preferably the book.

Carr, Clay. *The Competitive Power of Constant Creativity.* New York: AMACOM, 1994. Describes how an organization can institutionalize creativity rather than encourage and depend upon the creativity of isolated individuals.

————. *Teampower.* Englewood Cliffs, N.J.: Prentice Hall, 1992. Discusses the characteristics of successful teams and the competencies required to successfully manage teams.

————. "7 Keys to Successful Change," *Training* magazine, February 1994, pp. 55–60.

Csikszentmihalyi, Mihaly. *Beyond Boredom and Anxiety: The Experience of Play in Work and Games.* San Francisco: Jossey-Bass, 1977. The first book on some of the most significant research done on human motivation over the past three decades.

————. *The Evolving Self: A Psychology for the Third Millennium.* New York: HarperCollins, 1993. More philosophic than the other two works, it also recognizes the potential harm that his discoveries could cause.

————. *Flow: The Psychology of Optimal Experience.* New York: Harper & Row, 1990. Updates his research and presents it in a more popular, readable style. This is the book to start with.

Davidow, William H., and Michael S. Malone. *The Virtual Corpo-*

ration: *Structuring and Revitalizing the Corporation for the 21st Century.* New York: HarperCollins, 1992.

Garson, Barbara. *The Electronic Sweatshop: How Computers Are Transforming the Office of the Future into the Factory of the Past.* New York: Simon and Schuster, 1988. An extremely pessimistic book about the uses of computers in organizations, based on extensive interviews by the author.

Gould, Stephen Jay (ed.). *The Book of Life: An Illustrated History of the Evolution of Life on Earth.* New York: W. W. Norton, 1993. Besides being a leading paleontologist, Gould writes with tremendous clarity and style. Anything he writes is worth reading. This work is as good an introduction to evolutionary theory on the whole as you're apt to find.

————. *The Panda's Thumb: More Reflections in Natural History.* New York: Norton, 1980. Another one of the many, many books Gould has written on evolutionary theory.

Ingrassia, Paul, and Joseph B. White. *Comeback: The Fall & Rise of the American Automobile Industry.* New York: Simon and Schuster, 1994. Certainly one of the most entertaining and informative business books published in 1994.

Ishikawa, Kaoru. *What Is Total Quality Control?: The Japanese Way.* Translated by David J. Lu. Englewood Cliffs, N.J.: Prentice Hall, 1985. If you want to know what TQC or TQM was meant to be, this is where it begins. It remains a much better introduction to the core of TQM than most subsequent books on the topic.

Jantsch, Erich. *The Self-Organizing Universe: Scientific and Human Implications of the Emerging Paradigm of Evolution.* Oxford: Pergamon, 1980. If you want to understand the intricacies of self-organization from the molecular level up, this will tell you.

Kearns, David T., and David A. Nadler. *Prophets in the Dark: How Xerox Reinvented Itself and Beat Back the Japanese.* New York: Harper Business, 1992. A very honest look at the remaking of Xerox, written by the company's ex-CEO and his primary adviser. If you don't have firsthand experience with the impact of transformational or cultural change, this will provide it for you.

Mager, Robert, and Peter Pipe. *Analyzing Performance Problems, or You Really Oughta Wanna.* 2nd ed. Belmont, Calif.: Lake Publishing, 1984.

Mintzberg, Henry. *The Rise and Fall of Strategic Planning.* New York: Free Press, 1994. North America's most famous contrarian management thinker is at it again. He doesn't think much of traditional strategic planning; the book explains why.

National Center on Education and the Economy. *America's Choice: high skills or low wages!* Rochester, N.Y.: 1990. Perhaps the single best description of the relationship between schools and the needs of contemporary business. However, other studies have reached differing conclusions.

Ohmae, Kenichi. *The Mind of the Strategist: Business Planning for Competitive Advantage.* New York: Viking Penguin, 1983. One of the first attacks on centralized strategic planning.

Porter, Michael. *Competitive Advantage: Creating and Sustaining Superior Performance.* New York: Free Press, 1985. One of the classic books on competitive advantage.

Quinn, James Bryan. *Intelligent Enterprise: A Knowledge and Service Based Paradigm for Industry.* New York: Free Press, 1992. One of the several books extolling the "virtual organization," this one has a reasonably solid research base.

Schaffer, Robert H. *The Breakthrough Strategy: Using Short-Term Successes to Build the High Performance Organization.* New York: Harper & Row, 1988. A whole book devoted to describing a strategy similar to that outlined at the end of this book.

Schwartz, Peter. *The Art of the Long View.* New York: Doubleday Currency, 1991. To the extent that "scenario planning" is a viable form of long-range planning, this is the bible for it.

Semler, Ricardo. *Maverick: The Success Story Behind the World's Most Unusual Workplace.* New York: Warner Books, 1993. You won't really know how organizations can evolve effectively until you read this book.

Senge, Peter M. *The Fifth Discipline: The Art & Practice of the Learning Organization.* New York: Doubleday, 1990. You have read this already, haven't you?

Stack, Jack. *The Great Game of Business.* New York: Doubleday/ Currency, 1992. The author's philosophy on how to remake a company.

Treacy, Michael, and Fred Wiersema. *The Discipline of Market*

Leaders: Choose Your Customers, Narrow Your Focus, Dominate Your Market. Reading, Mass.: Addison-Wesley, 1995.

Zuboff, Shoshana. *In the Age of the Smart Machine: The Future of Work and Power*. New York: Basic Books, 1988. Based on several in-depth case studies, the author contrasts automating a process with "informating" it. Her hopeful conclusion that organizations need to do the latter, using the skills of their workers in the process, is not borne out by all the case studies presented.

Index